THE POWER
TO
MAKE MONEY$$

By

Cash McCall

**DEDICATED
TO**

Diane Powell

**My Very Good Friend
When I Needed Her Most,
She Was There For Me!**

**ALSO DEDICATED
IN MEMORIAM
TO**

GEORGE A. KEMPLAND

**Author, Friend, And So Very Much More
1929 — 2013
Wherever You Are Now, George,
*May You Always Be Happy, At Peace,
And Enjoying Yourself.
I Hope I May Get To See You Again…
Some when***

THE POWER TO MAKE MONEY
PUBLISHED BY: GKRS Publications
Copyright © 2020
By
Rob Shelsky

This is a work of nonfiction. The author acknowledges the trademarked status and trademark owners of various products referenced in this work of nonfiction, which have been used without permission. The publication/use of these trademarks is not authorized, associated with, or sponsored by the trademark owners. All quoted material and illustration/pictures are public domain.

Edition License Notes:

*****

CONTENTS

INTRODUCTION

Money! There are many of us, the majority, (the 99 Percent?), who could use more money and don't we know it, especially in such times as these! As one famous celebrity once said, "Money may not buy everything, but what it can't buy, I don't want!" That's an extreme, of course, but let's be honest. Most of us, the 99 percent of us, could definitely use more money. Money may not buy happiness, but it will buy nice homes, beautiful cars, and college educations, not to mention comfortable retirements and wonderful vacations, among other things.

Here's the truth of the matter; we would like the freedom such wealth brings us, the independence it buys, the benefits it allows each of us to have for ourselves and to help others we love, as well. The problem is...how do we get it? Money, as the saying goes, is not easy to come by. If it were, you wouldn't be reading this book!

The Power To Make Money will give you the answers you need, the steps to follow to make money. These aren't impossible steps necessitating that you jump through hoops or live like a pauper. They don't require you to take great risks with any money you might have now.

In fact, this guide doesn't require you to do anything illegal, immoral, or again, to "jump through any hoops" of any sort to obtain your financial goals. You don't need to follow a guru, any sort of preacher or teacher, or to reshape your entire personality and adopt some New Age view of the universe in any new way, in order to have "money flow" to you, as some of them put it. You just have to follow the simple steps outlined in this book. These are simple and easy steps. They are straightforward.

First and foremost, *The Power To Make Money* is a practical guide to obtaining your monetary goals. Because not all people have the same level of income, background, or opportunities, this book will be divided into sections geared, generally, to a number of such different income and background levels. You just have to pick the one that best suits you. But first, ask yourself this basic question:

Do You Need Money? This may sound like a stupid question, but it isn't. There are over seven billion people on this planet and counting. Although, we have much in common with each other, we have much that is different about our lives, as well. Sometimes, these differences are major.

For instance, there are those of us, although probably NOT the majority, but still there are many, who have no need for much money. At least, they have no need for great amounts of it. They don't want money in any large quantity, nor would they be likely to use it, or even be able to hang on to it, if they had it. This group includes certain religious sects who disdain the need for material possessions, as well as individuals and some others who simply are content with their current lot in life.

For many, as long as they have a roof over their heads, reasonable clothes to wear, and food on the table, they are satisfied for themselves and often for their families. That's fine...for them. I just hope that it is also fine for their immediate family members, as well, since they probably have no choice in the matter but to go along with the breadwinner's wishes. If the parents want to live in poverty, that's fine. It's their right. However, what about their children's rights? Do they automatically want to live in poverty, as well, to never have a chance to do anything special or fun, to never have the hope of going to college or university?

Whether someone is better off for not having much money or even none at all is a decision and philosophical question each person must make and answer for themselves, and many times, this means they are doing this for their closest relatives, as well. Parents desires are inevitably visited upon their children. Again, if the parents choose poverty, the child will have it, as well, by sheer default. Even so, when it comes to money, again, each must choose for themselves. Nobody else can do this for them. They must decide on an individual basis. Of course, the consequences can be great. One may not want money, but one's children might want a chance at a better life!

Is It Right To Want Money? Some argue that "money is the root of all evil." Others counter this by saying, "the lack of money is the root of all evil." Regardless of which group may be ultimately right about this, one thing is certain; the very rich, the so-called "One Percent," aren't going to give their money away to any of us any time soon! Moreover, they all seem to want their money well enough! Yes, they may give away billions to charity, but they aren't bankrupting themselves in the process. I've yet to hear of a single billionaire who gave away absolutely everything and went to live like a hermit on some mountaintop!

Ask yourself; why is that? Moreover, whether or not they should even do this is also not the point of this book. This book is not about the redistribution of wealth. It is about you making your own money, not about you getting it from someone else.

Please understand that the philosophical and moral aspects of whether making money is a good or bad thing, whether one should share it or not, are not subjects for debate here, not our concern. This book leaves such weighty ethical matters for others who are better qualified to determine such things. The sole purpose here, the whole point of this book is to show you how to make money and make it quickly. After all, without money, one doesn't even need to consider such questions of ethics or morality about wealth, not if one doesn't have any! It is only those not living in abject poverty who can "afford" to say that money isn't everything! Remember that.

Making Money for Those Who Want It.

Again, let me make this very clear; this book is about making money! Nothing more, but nothing less. It's that simple. *The*

Power To Make Money is about achieving this goal the quickest way possible and is meant to be a practical guide to achieve this end, that of making money. The topics included here, among others are:

—**Obtaining financial independence and getting out of debt,**

—**Obtaining the lifestyle we want for ourselves and those who depend upon us,**

—**Having opportunities to do what we want and when we want,**

—**Not waiting decades for our dreams to come true, but rather to achieve them far more swiftly,**

—**To retire early if we so choose, or even make it possible for us to retire at all,**

—**Having more time to do the things we want, rather than to do the things we have to do!**

—**To be able to buy time, that which is the very stuff of life. Billionaires buy the entire lifetimes of thousands of people in the form of money. So money is time!**

Sounds great, doesn't it? However, how do we go about doing this? Let me say this once more: If we want money, if we want the financial security that comes with it, the independence it gives us, as well as all the countless opportunities it affords us by having it, we can't count on anyone else, let alone that One Percent to just hand it over to us. They won't, trust me! Therefore, our only legal alternative is that we must make it for ourselves. As most of us know, that's not the easy part, especially if we want to achieve this goal in just a few years' time rather than a lifetime or even lifetimes!

For Whom Is *The Power To Make Money* Intended?

This book is for those who want and need to get ahead, who want a practical guide to become financially independent, to get out of debt, even to get "rich" or perhaps just have enough to comfortably retire early on, or even be able to retire at all. In short, this book is for anyone who wants to "get ahead," and to realize their financial dreams.

For example, baby boomers, along with many of those of the

younger generation coming after them, for many of these people, even the possibility of retirement is becoming just a wishful dream these days. A "good" retirement is fast becoming just a remote hope, a splendid daydream, and one getting ever more remote with the passing of time; such is the state of the current economy.

Don't want to wait? Don't want to have to just dream of a better tomorrow? Then this book is for you, for those who don't want to wait forever to get ahead!

What You Will Find In *The Power To Make Money*. The short answer is you will find out how to make money and as much of it as you want. You will find out how to do this, to attain your goals in a reasonable length of time, often just a matter of few years, but with real results beginning often in just a matter of a few weeks! Yes, your income can increase that quickly! This book will show you how.

Want to be financially independent?
Want to be free of outstanding debt?
Want more income?
Want to be able to afford more?

Well, as the saying goes, "you will never get rich by working for others," unless of course, you are at the top end of your profession already, as in being a CEO for a large corporation, a famous and sought after surgeon, or a billionaire tech wizard, financier, etc. Let's face it; most of us, the vast majority are simply not in any of those categories.

Moreover, let's be honest here, those people don't need this book. You do! If you picked this volume up at your local bookstore, or are reading this introduction online, it's for a reason. That reason is you want and need more money! Even now, if you are glancing through this introduction, then this book is definitely for you!

Hate your job? This book will help free you from having to work for anyone but yourself.

Hate your low level of income? *The Power To Make Money* will help you achieve whatever level of income you might want, and to do it rapidly. Using this book, you will see how swiftly and positively your income will change for you.

Once more, just to make it clear: **<u>this book is meant as a practical guide. It is a series of simple and practical steps you can apply to your own unique situation in order to get ahead and achieve those financial goals you have always dreamt of obtaining.</u>**

Simply apply the steps given in *The Power To Make Money* to your situation, your dreams and goals. Almost immediately, within just a few weeks, you should see improvements in your financial status if you follow these steps.

Some of the more cynical readers of this introduction might be thinking, "Yeah, I can see how the author made his money… by writing this book." You know what? They would be partially right! As we shall see, we each can take our own paths to accruing wealth by using the following practical guide. However, writing is not how I managed to retire at the age of 35, as you will see.

Writing is a path this author chose after early retirement, but it was hardly the only one! There were other methods that came before this one, and they will be shared with you, as well, to act as positive and reinforcing examples.

You see, *this book is not how the author is turning his life around.* That has already happened for him. Yes, any proceeds from *The Power To Make Money* will add to his income, of course, but writing wasn't what made him his money in the first place.

No, this book is about you turning your life around, about you getting ahead!

Following the simple steps outlined in this book helped the author to make his money, achieve his dreams. Those steps allowed him the income to have the TIME to write this book in the first place, and not having to take years to do it, because of only being able to write in small amounts between working two exhausting jobs just to pay the bills as he once did, as so many people have to do these days right now.

This brings up yet another point and this is an important one; by achieving wealth and/or financial independence, again,

ONE BUYS TIME. One suddenly has time to do those things they wanted to do for years, even perhaps yearned to be able to do, but couldn't afford. Whether going on extreme sports vacations, traveling Europe or wherever, taking up painting (and yes, writing), playing golf, or you name it, MONEY BUYS YOU TIME TO DO THESE THINGS!

As the plaque at the entrance to the Twelve Oaks Plantation in the movie, *Gone With The Wind*, read: "*Time is the stuff of life. Do not squander it.*"

Don't squander what time you have left, because as another old quotation says, "Time is money." Put your time to use to make money, lots of it! This book will show you how. Then, once you've accomplished your monetary goals, you will be free to spend the rest of your time on whatever you want and to do so for the rest of your life.

One Caveat: This must be very clear to the potential reader: this book is not about trying to give you a philosophy or new faith of any sort in order to make money or anything else of such a nature. Enough other books do that already, and I have to ask if you've read them, then:

How's that been working for you?

Are you rich now? If so, why are you reading this introduction?

No, *The Power To Make Money* is not written to convince you to have faith in anything, not even in the capitalistic monetary system, or any other system, for that matter. Nor is *The Power To Make Money* any sort of guide to you becoming a better person, a different person, or to make you acquire an "ism" or set of beliefs that will make money somehow magically fall into your hands from out of the universe.

There is no religious or spiritual element to this book in any way. That's not to say the author has anything against those sorts of things. In fact, they can be very helpful to a person trying to get ahead. Faith is a powerful thing. Still, having faith is not the point of this book, except perhaps, to have faith in yourself that you can do this, that you can make money!

Yet, one more time; *The Power To Make Money* is a simple, practical hands-on guide to getting started making money! Again, follow the steps outlined in the coming chapters and you will begin making money in the first few weeks of having read this book! There is no magic to this. There is no having to apply principles, or belief systems of any sort to accomplish your goals. These are just logical and sensible steps for you to take to make money and make it quickly.

Caveats, Tips, Examples, And More. In addition to the steps to making money, from time to time, the author will include caveats (warnings), tips as to how to do certain things more easily, as well as real-life examples of these. However, remember, these are just the author's personal opinions and experiences on such topics, but they could prove valuable to anyone starting out in wanting to make money.

Moreover, when it comes to money, why wait decades just to obtain a meager benefit from a life of overwhelming effort to gain just a small pittance at the end of it, a mere survival-level existence for your few remaining years? Nobody wants just to survive. Almost all of us want to live!

With *The Power To Make Money*, you will have the opportunity to do just that, to live! Moreover, if you follow the precepts in this book, you could live well! And remember, I'm not a stock broker, financier, financial consultant, or anything of the sort. I'm just someone, very much like you, who wanted to get ahead. I hope by sharing this, showing this guide to making money, it will help you, too! Now, let's get started.

CHAPTER ONE

*Step 1 —Is This What You
Want And How Badly?*

**STEP 1 TO MAKING MONEY: Decide How Badly You Want
Money.**

Is This What You Really Want? This may sound strange as a
step, but it is probably the most important one because it
concerns your level of motivation. The old saying, "act in
haste and repent at leisure" may be a cliché, but it is a true one.
Before you jump into trying to follow the remaining steps in this
book, you first need to carefully consider if this is truly something you want to do. Again, we could all use more money, would
like the benefits it brings, but as the author, Robert Heinlein once
said, "There ain't no such thing as a free lunch." He believed in
this so strongly that in a number of his books, he used a term
he coined, "TANSTAAFL," ("There Ain't No Such Thing As A Free
Lunch") to illustrate the importance of this point.

The idea is simple enough. No matter what we think we get for
free, no matter how easy something appears to be, there is always
a price to pay. The same holds true for making money just as much
as it does for anything else. There is a price to pay…ALWAYS!

Making Money Will Take Your Time, your effort, your persistence, and more. Making money will mean other things will have
to give way in the short run, at least and to some extent. Time

spent doing other things, often fun things, as with going out with other people, such as spouses and/or children, as well as friends, will be one of those victims, at least to some degree. One has only so much time available to them, and as most of us know, there is usually little left over as it is, even for those things we have to do.

Therefore, if you are to devote yourself to making money, you will quickly see that other things might have to be shelved for a while, other things you might enjoy doing by yourself or with others. Of course, there is a way to strike a balance with all this, but it takes some hard work to achieve this, some experimenting before such a balance in your life is achieved.

So how important to you is that weekend golf game, or that Saturday fishing trip, or perhaps more importantly, that son or daughter's ball game you'd like to attend? What about that date night with your spouse or significant other?

As always, there is only so much time in the day, and if you are serious about making money, much of that available time must go to that task. As much as we'd like to, we simply can't have it all or do it all…at least, not until we have the money to buy the time to do this.

You Are Going To Be Busy. Make no mistake about this. Furthermore, this means other things you like or need to do might have to "give way" at times. Your priorities will have to be re-arranged some, juggled, and make no mistake about it.

Consequently, you need to think carefully if this is really for you, making enough money to have what you want, to achieve your dreams, or instead, if you already have most of what you really want, and having more money is just "a nice idea." There are costs to achieving such goals. There always are. So be pragmatic. Think things through. Be sure you really want to "go for it," before you proceed.

Once having made this decision, and if it is to make money, then and only then proceed to the next step. But do give the matter careful thought first!

CHAPTER TWO

*Step 2 To Making Money —
The Starting Gate*

Taking Stock. The first thing we have to do is be utterly honest without ourselves here in our approach to making money. We must face things in a cold, practical, and realistic manner. We need to know exactly where we are starting from before we can take any action about our financial situation. As we all know too well, not everybody is at the same financial level, educational level, or social strata of society.

Yes, it would be great if circumstances of birth, upbringing, and education didn't matter, but they do. As most of us know too well, we don't all start life in the same position, at the starting point. Some are born with the proverbial "silver spoon" in their mouths and others (most of us) are not. I wasn't. This starting position in life necessarily affects your income producing capabilities and the length of time it might take to reach your financial goals. Therefore, the starting gate we initially come out of does matter in the race for wealth.

Do we all know what a "starting gate is?" Most of us probably do know, but for those who don't, the idea is very simple. A starting gate is the point on a racetrack, where racing horses or greyhound dogs, for instance, are lined up to begin a race. For animals, they are in a starting gate. For cars, people, bicycles, motorcycles, etc., it's just a starting line on the track, but the principle is the same.

A Better Starting Position. Here is the reason I belabor this simple point; certain racers, be they humans, animals, or cars, have a better starting position than others do. Those racers positioned in the starting gate or at the starting line *on the inside* of the track have less distance to travel to complete the distance around the circle than those on the "outside tracks." Hence, the use of the term, "he (or she) has the inside track to..." and this could be the inside track for a job, or whatever, as well. In other words, their chances are betting of winning because of their starting position.

Life in general is like that, as well. As we all know, life isn't fair, as much as we would like it to be. At least, it is not with regard to where and to whom we are born, where and how we are brought up, and how much money our families might have. In short, we are not born equal in those respects. Let me make this eminently clear:

Life Is Not A Level Playing Field!

Of course, this fact makes it tougher for some than it does for others to get ahead. Some of us are better positioned from birth, at the very outset of life to more easily achieve their dreams right from the very outset. They might have the right connections, too. Others, many of us, are not so lucky in this regard.

A Race To The Finish. Don't despair. Just because your starting position in life may be a poor one when it comes to making money and lots of it, this can change. Like any race, individuals can drop back from a favorable position while others in the rear might suddenly sprint ahead. Therefore, the concept of a starting gate in making money is a fluid thing, one that can change over time and individual circumstances. In other words, you can overcome your starting position in the race to make money.

Despite Life Not Being A Level Playing Field, You Can Still Make Lots Of Money!

However, where you are starting from, what assets you may or may not have in the way of material possessions, money, and/or a higher education may give you an advantage over others, or alternatively, reduce your abilities. Still, the principle here in *The Power To Make Money will* work and work well, no matter the initial circumstances of someone. Whether they are:

Blue-Collar Workers/Laborers. The definition of blue-collar workers has been:

"A working-class person historically defined by hourly rates of pay and manual labor. A blue collar worker refers to the fact that most manual laborers at the turn of the century wore blue shirts, which could hold a little dirt around the collar without standing out." [Blue Collar Definition/Investopedia]

In other words, this could include people who perform jobs that simply don't pay much, regardless of the skills that might be involved, and those paid hourly. This includes mechanics, farm laborers, home repairers, window washers, landscapers/gardeners, janitors, carpet cleaners, fast food/restaurant workers, teachers' aids, and many, many more besides.

Skilled, Semi-Professionals, And Professionals Who Are Often At The Low End Of The Pay Scale. Whether linemen for the county as the song goes, nurses, floor finishers, teachers, professors, plumbers, carpenters, roofers, technical and/or medical assistants, etc., secretaries, or white collar workers, there are many in this category who definitely could use more money.

Young People Just Starting Out. With college costs reaching truly astronomically high levels, many young people simply can't afford to go to college, or to get the training they might like to have to advance themselves. This means that despite their possible talents, they are often stuck in dead-end jobs that pay little and have little opportunity for advancement.

A great or even brilliant future is closed to them, cut off, for all practical purposes. We all know of young people in this category, I'm sure. There are others, those not lucky enough even to finish high school, which are in the same circumstances, or even worse ones. Of course, they could use more money. We all could!

Young People Who Are In Debt, Perhaps Due To Student Loans.

There are many students who have attended college/university, and who have graduated. Nonetheless, they are no better off in many cases than those who didn't go to university, because they are now burdened with heavy and long-term student loans they must pay off—student debts.

Sometimes these debts are for years and even decades to come. This means that many of them will reach middle age before they even clear such student loans and so have little or no chance of accruing any personal wealth in the meantime, or far less than they might otherwise have obtained in those years of paying student loans. The sad part is that they can't even declare bankruptcy in order to clear such student loan debts, because student loans are exempt from such bankruptcies.

Middle-Aged And Older People. Many people who are middle aged or even older may be in severe financial straits. The Great Recession may have destroyed their savings, wiped out their jobs or forced them to take lower paying ones, and even forced them to give up their homes, and more!

These people are now struggling along, year after year, often working at jobs that pay far less than the ones they once had and with no hope of a brighter future, early retirement, or even any retirement at all. They might dream of someday owning a home again, but realistically, know time is fast running out for them to accomplish such a goal. The clock is ticking!

In addition, with the economy still stumbling along in many ways, even years after the Great Recession and now thanks to the pandemic, perhaps slipping into a Great Depression, their prospects of again regaining what they once had seem unlikely. At least they do, **if they are relying on working at a standard job to get there! They may be lucky to even have a job in the next few years!** The pandemic and resulting financial collapse of our economy does not bode well for things in the near term.

Therefore, You Absolutely Must Face Reality With Regard To Your Current Financial Conditions If You Want To Improve Them. Why am I saying all this? Well, because it is just so important for us to realize our current situation, the financial predicament we are now in. Recognizing our current reality is the first step to making money! And by the way, this guide will be geared to those classifications listed above:

Blue-Collar Workers/Laborers

Skilled, Semi-Professionals, And Professionals Who Are Often At The Low End Of The Pay Scale

Young People Just Starting Out

Young People Who Are In Debt, Perhaps Due To Student Loans

Middle-Aged And Older People

The advice here should apply to all of them. Again, some of us just are not in the same position as others. Why is this important? Because being this is reality, your (1) position at the starting gate will affect how long it takes you to reach your goals and there is no point in denying that. This is for two reasons:

a. You may be starting with much less in the way of assets to begin your trek toward wealth than others, and

b. Your goals may be higher and so might take longer to reach, regardless of your starting position. The higher the goals, the more money you want to make, the longer it will take. This is just a basic fact.

And (2), the current economic circumstances may have negatively impacted you.

Don't Let This Discourage You! If you keep following the steps in this book, you will still make money and make it quickly; again, this usually starts in just a matter of weeks if you follow the guidelines. You simply might not make as much money and as speedily as someone else might, but that doesn't matter. You aren't interested in "someone else" making money. You are only interested in how much and how swiftly you can make it for yourself.

A. Your Sole Goal Should Be Your Interest In You Making Money For Yourself. You must be single-minded in this endeavor. Therefore, when approaching the idea of making money, the first step, as stated above, is to take a realistic look at your situation, with all the dimples and warts your position at the starting gate might give you.

Don't lie to yourself. Don't pretend. Avoid self-delusion about the state of your finances, as in pretending to something you are not, or simply don't really have. For example, you may have a decent income and an expensive home and so think you are fairly well off.

However, if your mortgage is greater than the house is worth, if you are "upside down" in the home's value versus the mortgage, and it's a large monthly mortgage at that, that's not an asset. It's a liability, so don't lie to yourself or pretend otherwise. Despite looking like you are well off, having a nice home and a decent income, you may in fact, not be! That's the real situation, although as you drive up to your big home in your nice car, it might seem otherwise to you, but that is just self-deception and self-delusion.

Meanwhile, someone with much less in the way of owning such things might actually be better off than you are at the starting gate, especially if they don't have much in the way of outstanding debts. Their starting position may not have the burden of a huge mortgage, a white elephant of a home or expensive car. I personally know people who have car payments larger than their mortgage payments, for example. **Therefore, Steps 1 and 2 to start making money, are to take a very realistic look at your situation and then your starting position.**

Again, don't hide the facts from yourself about your current financial/economic state.

Don't imagine things are better than they are, or for that matter, worse than they are.

I can't stress how important this is as a step to making money. As an example of this last, of someone thinking they are actually worse off than they are, I had a friend who was close to retirement. Being good friends, we talked a lot. One day, I said to him, "When you retire, you will be able to finally do what you really want." This was because he was complaining about his job, which he often did.

Then one day, when I said this yet again, he snapped angrily back at me, "When I retire? Don't you get it? I can never afford to retire. I have a mortgage, car loan, and too much else to ever hope to retire any time soon."

This got me to thinking about his situation. He was older than I was and I understood he didn't want to go on working forever. He was 53 going on 54, and so was of an age when most people begin readying themselves for retirement, or even early retirement. However, he felt the situation was hopeless. He didn't think he could ever afford to retire, let alone do so early!

NOT SO! I asked if he would share all his financial information with me. He was willing and so I went over his situation. I approached the problem in a realistic, pragmatic manner, rather than an emotional one, because I wasn't emotionally bound up in it as he was. I had no stake in the outcome, other than to try to help a friend in trouble.

Again, many people find it hard to look at their personal situations in a realistic manner. Some don't want to look at it at all, as if by not doing so, the problem will just go away. Some hide the truth from themselves because it is unpleasant, while others simply can't see a way out, even though there might well be one. They consider the situation so hopeless, there would be no use in even bothering. This is understandable but it is also counterproductive. If you can't face your monetary situation, then you won't be able to take the necessary steps to improve it.

Therefore, the first thing I did was to be realistic with regard to his situation. I asked him to be a little more detailed about his current financial state. When he finished doing this, having his financial status and his relative position at the starting gate for making money, I then moved on to what became the third step for making money....

CHAPTER THREE

The Second Step — Taking
Actual Stock

THE THIRD STEP TO MAKING MONEY:

This step should hardly be a surprise to anyone, because it is so basic. Having first determined to be realistic about your actual financial status, and so then examining it, the next obvious step in this case, is to take stock of your assets and liabilities, what you have going for you and what you financially have against you when it comes to making money.

At this point, you should make a list. Include in the list your liabilities, those financial burdens you carry. For some, this is an understandably depressing thing to have to do and that's why we stressed being realistic in the last chapter. You just have to do this. It is a fundamental necessity to making money—taking stock of your assets and liabilities.

Yes, for those in heavy debt, this is a disheartening task, assuredly. After all, one could well be in a situation where all they have, in their own estimation, is debt. Furthermore, they might feel they have nothing at all in the way of assets to balance all that debt.

Having been in that very desperate situation a while back, I know exactly how one can feel about being hopelessly in debt, of not being able to find any way out of that dark tunnel of financial obligation. Yes, it was a heavy debt. **I had some $50,000 in credit card debt**!

Therefore, I know firsthand how such a monumental task as to face taking stock can be. I know from bitter personal experience. Moreover, you may think you have nothing going for you in that regard, no redeeming feature to counter all that debt. I know that I felt that way at the time.

NOT SO! You have you! Most people don't even realize they have this or that it is even an asset. If you have the determination to get out of debt and then to go on to achieve your financial dreams, you can do it! I'm not saying this as some sort of "pie-in-the-sky" hope, just to help sell this book, but rather because it's true!

Furthermore, if you bought this book, it says one thing about you right away: **YOU ARE SERIOUS ABOUT MAKING MONEY**. So you already have one asset—you! Now make a list of any other assets you might have, as well. You have others. For some, it is income from a job. For others it may be equity in one's home. For yet others it might be a powerful interest in a hobby or avocation that might make you money, as well. And there are other such assets. List them and do the same for your liabilities. But remember, you are an asset to yourself.

The Ultimate Secret To The Power To Make Money. Additionally, and unlike so many books about getting rich that wait until the very end to do the "big reveal" of their "secret for success,"

I'll tell you right now, what the secret to *The Power To Make Money* is. It is you! It's that simple. You need nothing more to achieve your goals than you!

It is your being determined that you want to have it all, or at least to have what will make you happy and content. That's it! There's nothing more to it than that. There is no magic formula, no secret potion, or as mentioned earlier, no "big reveal" to all this. It's simply you, a determined you, one who wants to make money, have a better life, and wants to get doing it right now!

Now let's move on: You already have the first three steps. I will repeat them here: You have to have what I would call a brutally realistic approach to your circumstances. Again, don't lie to yourself! Look at your personal situation as honestly and objectively as you can. Take stock of your debts and assets. List them. In this instance, it might help to have someone else who can be more objective about it, to do this with you. A friend, perhaps, a spouse or loved one, or even an acquaintance you implicitly trust. However, here I have a Major Caveat:

Beware of Debt Consultants. When it comes to trying to find aid via a debt consultant, be VERY careful. Personally, I don't recommend them as a usual thing to use.

Most of them are in the business to make money, even many of the so-called nonprofit ones. There are other nonprofit "charities" that do this, as well, that will phone you up and ask for donations to various worthwhile causes, but then keep as much as 80 percent or more of the donation for themselves and pass on only a fraction of the total you give them to the actual charity involved. Do they help these charities? Yes, they do, but they really help themselves, as well, and at your expense. Get it?

The same holds true for many so-called debt consultants. After all, they have to make a living, too…and guess at whose expense that will be? Yes, you again! My personal advice is generally to avoid debt consultants at the outset for this reason. First, many expect to be paid, or have a stake in hooking you up with so-called "debt relief consultant agencies." Although there are those who are reputable and helpful, of course, there are also way too many predator types out there, as well.

An inexperienced and desperate person can easily fall prey to these people, and far too often, they do! Any consultant who in any way charges you for their help is not helping the bottom line of your debt burden. Well, let's be honest here; are they? Aren't their charges, their fees, their percentages, or whatever, just adding to your total debt? This means it will take even longer to get out from under such a heavy financial burden. And a great deal of their advice is public domain knowledge already.

Again, this is not to say there aren't any reputable aid groups and debt consultants out there. Of course, there are. There are consultants who are genuine and helpful. Nevertheless, unless you are certain you are dealing with a true, nonprofit organization in every sense, again, my personal advice is to avoid debt consultants. If they are charging you for their help, that's not a good sign to begin with!

Another Caveat: Even many so-called "nonprofit" debt consultants, who might not charge fees for consulting with you, could then afterwards charge for supposedly aiding you in talking down debts with your debtors. I've heard more horror stories about this sort of thing.

People have told me tales where the person who hoped a debt consultant would help them out of debt, only succeeded in pushing them further into debt. Some poor souls get strung along for months paying fees to consultants for such services, expecting the consultant to act as a go-between with financial companies they owe money to. And no debt relief ever materialized! In short, they paid for help with renegotiating their debts for financial relief, but never achieved this goal. Why? Because that consultant never lifted a finger to contact such financial institutions! If the debt consultant takes money, but can offer "no guarantees," then watch out!

Once more, my personal opinion and it is just that and no more, is that you take your own realistic look at your financial situation, again, either by yourself or with someone you can trust, a spouse, partner, good friend, or relative. After all, a debt consultant has no more power to renegotiate a debt any better than you do. Either can pick up a phone just as easily and make a call. Moreover, many corporations, such as banks and financial institutions don't even want to deal with debt consultants.

The truth is you might be better off just hiring a lawyer, instead, but again, this will also cost you! Furthermore, it could cost you big time! Remember, you want to lower your debt and not increase it. And for some reason, when dealing with lawyers on such issues, the results can seem to take a VERY long time to materialize. Not always, but often enough to make me wary of personally going that route. However, if you wish to declare bankruptcy, or something on that order, then I strongly recommend and attorney to help you.

Now that you understand the need for a realistic approach and why it is necessary to be careful as the first step, what should you do next?

Taking Stock of Your Situation, First, Your Debt. Now, how actually to go about doing this is simple. Start with your debts. You don't need to know to the penny what you owe, just a good approximation. How do you do this? Simple:

1. Check all your bills to find the total debt outstanding on them. Most bills will show you not only what your next monthly payment is, but also the total amount still due.

2. If your bills don't give you the outstanding total owed, call the company in question and ask. Often this information is part of their automated phone response system, as an item you can pick from their phone menu. Usually, it's under the category of "balance." In any case, it is a quick and easy thing to do to get the total you owe on something.

3. Write down the totals still owed on all your bills. Include car payments, but not the house payment at this point (that is, if you own a home and have a mortgage on it). Note the total amount of what is owed on your mortgage, but do not include it in the total you are going to make of all credit card debt, car payment debt, any other debts owed for furniture, appliances, student loans, etc. **ALL DEBT BUT ANY MORTGAGE PAYMENT ON YOUR HOUSE SHOULD BE INCLUDED IN TOTALING YOUR DEBTS!** We will return to the matter of a home mortgage later on in this book.

4. Now, if you haven't already, total all that debt. Again, remember, this does NOT include a home mortgage payment. Write the total down so you don't forget it.

There is often a shock when a person realizes just how much they really owe. There was for me when I realized it was just over $50,000, I assure you! Again, it's better to know the truth than to just mentally fudge the figures to something less than they truly are to make yourself feel better. Even so, realizing the extent of one's debt is often a bitter pill to swallow. However, if you are going to rid yourself of debt, you have to know just how much that amount really is.

Now List Your Assets. Having totaled your debt, now you have to take stock of your assets. Yes, you may feel you have very little of these, but again, remember, you have you! That's no small asset. Again, it's the biggest one you can have. What constitutes assets? Anything that adds to your total worth, or might add to your income. Here are some examples:

Your job. Income from your job is an asset, of course. You weekly/monthly pay is an asset.

You home. Whether you own a home outright, or have equity in it, this can also be an asset, that is if you aren't bottom up in debt (where you owe more money on it than the house is now worth).

Any other income you may have. Whether in the form of stocks, bonds, part-time job income, income from hobbies, etc., these are all assets. Yes, I know that when one is broke that it isn't likely they will have stocks and bonds. I didn't. Still, some people do and sometimes, these pay dividends, which is income and so can help, even as the stocks and bonds themselves would be assets.

Physical saleable items. Do you have any extra vehicles, boats, tractors, jet skis, portable home generators, art, or any material goods that might actually bring you something if sold? You might be surprised what you have in this way. I know people who said they had nothing, and then it turned out they had all sorts of items they could sell off and not even miss, such as bicycles their kids no longer used, rototillers, pressure washers, etc.

One woman even had a complete set of antique Limoges china, including all the accessory pieces, and this was worth thousands of dollars! She never used the set. Her mother had handed it down to her.

However, don't sell anything you really need or love, but take a hard look at things. It was tough for this woman to sell the china because of its sentimental value, but really, how sentimental was it, when she had the entire set boxed away under a bed and she never even looked at it! One can always keep one special piece, place it in a prominent position in a display case, and then have that serve as the focus of sentimental value.

The important thing here is that the woman's mother would probably have preferred her daughter to be all right financially, to be able to live a decent life, rather than continue in debt and poverty while having boxes of unused china under her bed that were worth a small fortune!

A case in point; I also knew an impoverished aristocrat from Europe. He had no money left, was in debt (in fact, I let him live at my house for a year at a reduced rent rate just to help him), but he had many antiques, and valuable items.

His grandmother always told him that as beautiful as the things were (paintings, furniture, *objets d'art*, etc.) that they were in reality, just things. If he ever needed to sell them, he should. This, he finally did. With the resulting income from the sale of such items through a leading world auction house, he bought his own home and started traveling again, because he could afford to do so once more.

He went from being broke, barely able to get by, and being elderly, afraid of dying in poverty and debt, to being well off and content. All it took was for him to decide that his personal wellbeing was more important than sentimentality. Moreover, he did keep a few special things just as remembrances of those who had gone before him, so it wasn't as if he had to sell everything!

So don't overlook any saleable items you may have for your list, whether a desert lot of land you've been hanging onto for years, or some valuable china, or whatever. Decide if you can part with them, if by selling them your life might be better for doing so. All of these things and more can be assets, help you to achieve your financial goals. Once you have finished taken stock, you now have a realistic picture of just how much you owe!

Yes, you knew you were in considerable debt, but now you KNOW exactly how much. This is necessary, because to have a goal, one must have a very explicit, very clear idea of just what that goal is, has to be.

Well, having taken stock it's time to move on. Now we go to the third step, and here's where we actually begin making money!

CHAPTER FOUR

The Fourth Step —Taking Control
Of Your Income

Reducing Outgo Means Increasing Income!

This is a big one! Remember at the beginning of this book that I stated you could begin increasing your income in just a matter of few weeks? Well, that statement was entirely true and in this chapter, I describe how you start to do just that! Income isn't just a matter of getting more money from new sources. Income is also a matter of getting more money from old sources, as well, and one of those ways is to cut the outflow of cash.

This way, you get to keep more of what you earn, or however you derive your income right now, simply by not losing so much of it in outgo spending.

Yes, you've probably heard it all before, about how to budget, limit your expenses, blah, blah blah. Most of us have even been given that advice at one time or another, that we should keep a record, a sort of journal or diary of every cent we spend for a month or two, to give us a better idea of just what we're "wasting" our money on. Although not bad advice at all, there are two major problems with this approach:

1. A lot of self-discipline and time is required to jot down every single item we spend money on all day long. This method takes a lot of work, diligence, and persistence. I have personally tried this at one point in the past when I was in financial trouble. After the first day, I gave it up as being just too cumbersome and time-consuming a method. I wanted to do it, but I just didn't have the time.

When you are standing in line to check out your groceries, for instance, other customers take a dim view of you hanging around to jot down the total costs. Even taking all those receipts home and then totaling them takes time and is, in my opinion, tantamount to daily bookkeeping. I'm just not cut out that way, to have to do that when I'm finally home from a long day of work. The idea of then having to sit down and totaling up a bunch of receipts daily is distinctly unappealing to me!

Not to mention (but I will), most of us always seem to be running late, so even stopping to do such a thing out in the parking lot of the store or at home isn't always an easy thing to accomplish. Kids screaming for dinner, wife or husband waiting on you, dog needing a walk, etc., all conspire to make taking time to jot down every little purchase sometimes very difficult! That's just life.

2. Many of us already have a good idea of where our money goes anyway and many of us want it to continue going "there" in some instances. There are those of us who stop for a Starbucks coffee every morning, as a sort of ritual on our way to work, for example. This is just one way we might be spending money, and we are fully aware of doing this.

However, have you ever considered just how much that one cup of Starbucks coffee is really costing you? USA Today has a "coffee calculator one can use, and it is based on a 16-ounce cup of coffee, just their (Starbuck's) regular house brand. Special blends can cost even more, as most of us know.

Here's how they say it works out:

As of the writing of this book, the cost of that **one cup a coffee from Starbucks a day will cost you $63.00 a month!**

This comes to approximately $756 a year! Already, that's a considerable amount. If used to pay a credit card debt, it would go quite a way to lowering it.

However, **keep this up for 30 years, and the total bill for just that single cup of coffee a day will cost $23,000, approximately!** Not so quite cheap sounding now, is it? Wouldn't that make a nice savings nest egg as you approach retirement age, or at least a heck of a good start on one, and all for the price of just that one cup of coffee a day?

Now let's do a little comparison again, using USA Today's calculator once more. This time, let's compare that cup of coffee, the same size, if made at home. Here's how that works out:

The cost per month will be just a measly $2.40 instead of the Starbucks $63.00.

The cost per year will be just $29.20 going that home-brewed route instead of that whopping $756 a year.

Finally, over a 30-year period, the cost of that one cup of coffee a day from home will equal just $876 instead of $23,000 if you instead purchased it at a Starbucks!

Let's be honest, a nest egg of just $876 isn't much to have at the time of retirement, but saving $22,124 (amount you'd save minus the cost of making that cup of coffee at home) and socking that amount away for old age or retirement isn't so bad!

However, there is more! The sooner that money goes into a bank account; the sooner it starts earning interest for you. If you add $726.80 a year (the amount you save each year by not going to Starbuck minus the cost of making that same cup of coffee at home), then **the amount at the end of 30 years, even if you only earned a measly 2.5% interest on your savings would have grown to $33,432.** Now that's getting to be a significant amount! And that's at a low interest rate. If you instead had invested the money each year in the stock market, the amount on average (based on the last 20 years of the stock market's performance, and it's average annual return over that time of 10 percent per year), your investment would be an astonishing **$132,236! A heck of an amount and all from just not buying a daily expensive cup of coffee! Under such a plan, you would have earned an astonishing $109,705 in interest alone!** This is based on interest being compounded annually.

Do I have your attention now? Of course, this is just a sample and is subject to how the economy performs over such lengthy periods of time, but the good news is that over such long-term periods, the stock market has consistently done about ten percent on average per year in profits, so keep that in mind! There are no guarantees, of course. Nothing is guaranteed in this life, but the odds are pretty good that if you started at 25 years of age doing this, you would end up with somewhere around that figure of **$132,236** by the age of 55!

And that's just doing this with one cup of coffee per day! Imagine if you made other cutbacks, as well, and cutbacks that didn't impact your quality of life. Eat a doughnut a day? Stop off for lunch every day at a fast food restaurant instead of bothering to make your own sandwiches or whatever? It all adds up, so it's not just that "lousy cup of coffee" we're talking about here!

Moreover, remember, you still get a darn good cup of coffee every day! **You aren't cheating yourself out of something you particularly desire. You are just going about it a different and much cheaper way!**

Something else to consider; that cup of coffee isn't going to stay at that same price forever. Chances are, over time, it will only keep going up, so think how much more you would save by not purchasing it!

Remember, lessen your outgo and increase your income!

I've had many people tell me that having that Starbucks (or whatever store brand one chooses—Starbucks is just an example and nothing more—I'm not picking on them) cup of coffee a day is important to them, that they really need to do it.

Do they? How badly do they need to do that? At $63 a month that would pay for a very decent cellphone service on a monthly basis, or even a decent cable television, satellite service, or Internet service. How about using it to make a monthly payment on credit card debt? Which do they need more; the store-bought cup of coffee or keeping their cellphone service active, or paying their debts?

Furthermore, using this method, nobody is doing without! They are still getting that cup of good coffee a day, and they can take it to work with them in a "special cup" if it makes them feel better about it. In doing so, they will have saved over $60 a month!

If that $60 a month isn't going out, then it is added income, money coming in! It's money available to be saved, invested, or used in some other positive way, as in paying down some debt. It's money that wasn't available to you before you changed your behavior.

In addition, $60 a month may not seem like a heck of a big leap in your income, but guess what? It will pay more than the minimum payment on practically any credit card that you might have a thousand dollars in debt on! Are you having trouble making those payments on time? Just start making your coffee at home, and taking it with you to work. That way, you will have your coffee and your credit card payment debt met, too! Get it?

It's all about how you use the money you have, folks!

Just saving the $60 or so a month may seem rather trivial to some people, but we're not just talking coffee here, either! We're talking all sorts of things people frivolously spend money on and all the time, and without thinking of it as more than just a trivial and infrequent expense.

Wrong!

Spending money on "trivial" items adds up, just as the interest debt on those outstanding credit cards you owe money on does, as well. How do you think credit card companies make their money? They make it through charging you interest on your debt. They know the value of interest, even if you don't! They make billions doing just that!

And so do billionaires. Have you ever looked at the spending habits of most billionaires? Did you know that on average they eat out a good deal less than the average working family? Were you aware that for most common purchases, they buy reliable brands but not designer brands in shoes, clothing, etc.? Labels aren't important to them, even if we've been taught that they should be important to us! We've been taught that for a reason—because labeled items cost more and it is those very billionaires that are making that extra money by convincing you of the fact that you must have that label.

For example, do you really think an IPhone is worth a thousand dollars? They are a great phone, no doubt, as is Samsung and others, but I have a phone that does just about everything those phones can do and it only cost me $187. Also, by going that route, it means I don't have to contract for a one-to-two-year plan that I can't get out of. Anyone who says that their iPhone or Samsung is free with "the plan" is kidding themselves. They are paying for it monthly, and at top dollar! **Remember, TANSTAAFL—"THERE AIN'T NO SUCH THING AS A FREE LUNCH!"**

So why do we buy $800 IPhones, and/or a $500 to $700 Samsung? Well, because we've been brainwashed into believing that we should. We've been told they are "the best." Not to mention, we do all love that snob appeal of having something others can't afford! And if you don't believe me, just do a little research on phones. You'll find there are great ones with wonderful features at a fraction of the cost of the top-billed ones!

So don't take my word for it. Check it out for yourself. And remember, those annual plans are designed to entice you into buying a new phone, whether you need it or not, every year or so, by just "rolling it over" in the plan. Oh, and don't forget phone insurance. With those expensive phones, you probably want it. Whereas, with a much cheaper phone, you don't need it! You just get another one, and the price of that phone will be less than the additional cost of the insurance you will pay for that expensive phone!

The whole system is guaranteed to make money for those selling the phones and it works! Apple has one of the largest, if not the largest reserve of cash of any company on Earth! Guess where all that cash came from? That's right, you and people like you!

So think about what happens when you don't practice such measures, as with that daily cup of coffee. Not only are you losing over $60 a month for that coffee you are buying on the way to work, but your credit card debt is going up each month in the meantime. You could be paying down on that debt with that extra $60, instead. You could be well on the way to financial success simply by using alternate methods of daily behavior practices. And nobody is asking you to go without! You don't have to become a monk or priest in the sense of taking a vow of poverty. You can still live a comfortable and very similar existence without all those high-priced, label items!

After all, you aren't a teenager anymore, and you should be well past the peer group pressure phase of having to have the "right phone," or "right pair of shoes," or "right jeans," or whatever! Grow up. Knock off the "keep up with the Jones'" behavior. Learning to control your spending habits is a part of that growing up, although the modern commercial world is intent on us not doing that. They want us to spend, spend, and spend some more! Why? Take a guess! Oh, yeah, it's so **THEY CAN MAKE THE MONEY AND NOT YOU!**

How many of us (myself included here), have bought something new because we were enticed into it by advertising and relentless commercial pressure. I have a perfectly good refrigerator. It's a double-door, large one, complete with water and ice dispenser, and it matches my kitchen just fine. (God forbid our appliances shouldn't all match, because we've been taught very carefully that they should!) However, a number of my friends began buying the refrigerator with the pull-out drawer freezer at the bottom. I've never like them. I don't like stooping over and rummaging while bent double every time I want something from a freezer. Yet, it was the latest thing at the time and everyone was buying them. Moreover, they average anywhere from $500 to over a $1,000 more than the standard double-door I had purchased.

Did I need such a refrigerator? No, of course not. Was it really any better than the one I had? No, it wasn't. In fact, in some ways, it was even worse. The computerized features on it, which told you what groceries needed replacement were a gimmick that I was quite sure I would never use. And by the way, did you know that those computerized extras have a very short lifespan and are very expensive to replace?

Your refrigerator may last 10 years, but most likely, those display add-ons won't! And now, some refrigerators even have water filters that won't allow you to get water out of your refrigerator's system if they are not replaced in a timely manner. They automatically shut down. And those filters cost! They can be as much as $50 in some instances.

So buy the more expensive refrigerator that really isn't better, along with those "necessary" water filters and whatever at high cost, and expect to have to make repairs or replace the refrigerator far sooner than you would have to with your older model? Not really a very astute financial thing to do, is it?

But they look so good to us in our kitchens, don't they? That's for about a week or a month at most! Then we stop noticing them! But you see, we have been convinced that we "need" these new features, and we "need" that new style, etc. The truth is, no we don't. We've just been taught that we do, and very carefully, too, through a lot of expensive advertising and developed peer group pressure!

Would you like some more examples? Well, the average American, as an adult individual, spends just about $232 a month eating food prepared outside the home, such as in eating out, or ordering in pizza or takeout, or whatever. The cost of the average large pizza, plus tax, delivery, and tips runs close to $30 these days, or more. That may seem cheap to feed a family, but it isn't really, not for one meal! Besides which, many go further and have to order those extra breadsticks, dessert pizza, soft drinks, or whatever.

Cha-Ching!

Up and up goes the cost of that pizza delivery (not to mention the price of the tip you pay the deliverer, because the higher the price, the greater the tip, usually. Oh, and don't forget that two-to-three dollar "delivery charge" the pizza chain adds on that is not part of the tip!).

In fact, recently and for the first time ever, Fox News stated that according to its numbers, **the average American family now**

spends more money per month on eating out than the cost of groceries for the entire month! This is incredible and yet many of us lament the fact we have a hard time "makings ends meet" financially. Gee, I wonder why?

And yet, when we buy a home, we just have to have that "gourmet style" kitchen, complete with all the expensive appliances like that new refrigerator, a kitchen we barely ever use!

Is it any wonder we're spending so much money unnecessarily? If nothing else, we're spending all our money on take out and restaurants! It may be convenient to do this, but it isn't cheap! And billionaires don't do it! That's why they are billionaires and we aren't! Get it again?

So if we base our cost estimates for one adult individual, we now have $292 a month in costs just for eating out periodically during any given month, and buying that one "treat" of a cup of coffee a day. Moreover, it doesn't end there. We pay out for cable/satellite TV, with many paying, on average, way over a $100 a month for just that convenience. We often "bundle" such services and can pay as much as $150 or more a month this way, too.

Combine this with the cost of eating out, those daily coffee "treats," and now we are in the neighborhood of $440 a month or more even much more! That's a car payment for many, and even a mortgage or rent payment for some! So is it worth it? Is it worth to bury ourselves in deeper and deeper debt just to live such a profligate and pointless lifestyle? Who are we trying to impress? Everybody is doing it, so it's not as if we're standing out from the crowd by doing it! It isn't making us "special" to do it. We're just one of many millions who have all fallen for the same thing.

It doesn't end there. People impulse buy all the time, candy, breath mints, soft drinks—whatever—we buy it. If you doubt this, go into any supermarket and just look at what lines each side of the checkout registers—all sorts of "stuff" that you might "just decide" to pick up while waiting in line there. Marketing experts know people buy things on impulse and that's why they jam the cash register lanes with shelves of impulse goods, "stuff" you normally wouldn't purchase.

They have researched this. They have carefully designed their markets to make you "add that one or two little extra(s)" even as you are about to leave the store! And it works! It works every day, all day long. Just stand and watch how many people pick up that little something extra while they are standing in the checkout line. While we're spending the money needlessly on impulses, the grocery stores are making it!

It doesn't stop there. Movie theaters pump the smell of fresh made popcorn into the lobby and theater itself to make us hungry and entice us to buy it. The same with the smell of coffee at coffee shops. All sorts of fast-food places exhaust the smell of their foods outside, such as that of fresh-baked pizzas, hot sandwiches...whatever it takes to attack us on the subliminal or subconscious level to become hungry and want to buy those items! And it works!

Again, most of us aren't up to keeping a journal of everything we buy and I think there is a reason why this is so; we just really don't want to know! We don't want to know how much money we are really spending and often so pointlessly. We'd rather stick to our fantasy that it is "within reason" rather than face the reality we're behaving like sheep or cattle and purchasing, as if in a trance, all this "stuff" we don't need.

Now to state the obvious; that kind of cash savings per month could go a long way to helping you meet your debt obligations and/or putting some money away in savings or investments of whatever sort. And those investments make even more money. And that's the whole point of this book—to make money, to acquire the power to do so!

Therefore, if you are doing this sort of thing with regard to such spending, as the "average American" who in debt is, then seriously consider ways to cut back on this. Every dollar you save is a dollar to pay off debts and save that interest, or to invest to make money! Rather than carrying an ever-increasing debt burden, spending all night worrying about possible bankruptcy, you might just get well off and wealthy, instead!

Mind you, I don't mean to "cut out" everything we enjoy. We

have to live for today as well as tomorrow. However, we have to be smart how we go about doing that. Buy a good grade of coffee and make it at home. Pour it into a traveling cup and take it with you, and no, saying you waste coffee that way, because you make more than you need is nonsense. It is still FAR CHEAPER, even wasting the excess coffee by the cupful or more on a daily basis, than it is to buy that cup of coffee at some chain of coffee houses or shops. The difference is still huge!

Oh, and avoid using those coffee machines that make just one cup at a time, but you have to purchase their "special" individual containers "pods," of coffee to do this. The cost of making coffee this way is FAR HIGHER than just buying ground coffee or coffee beans and grinding it yourself, which if you do, gives you a very robust and fresh-tasting coffee, and without extra chemical additives to make it do so.

Please understand, I'm not against Green Mountain or any other company selling coffee these ways, because they are convenient, do allow for more choice for each individual in a home to choose the blend they want each time they brew that single cup. I do object to their impact on the environment, though, because it isn't a good one, and it isn't small.

Still, don't kid yourself! One of the original producers of those coffee machines for single-cup brews recently coded their coffeemakers not to accept other and cheaper brands of good quality coffee pods.

Why? Just why are they doing this, exactly?

Because it makes them MORE MONEY! LOTS MORE! Their coffee pods are higher priced, so not only are they selling their own brands, but they are making a darn good profit in the process! Remember, that money they are making has to come from somewhere and it's coming from you if you have one of those machines! So, reconsider your daily practices and behavior patterns. They can cost you a fortune for no good reason!

By the way, so high priced and annoying is this new coding of their coffeemakers to "refuse" to accept other container brands, that people on the Internet are posting ways to get around it!

Moreover, sales of one of those brands of coffee machines have plummeted recently. That certainly says something about how people are reacting to this new "forcing" of them to buy a certain, and higher-priced brand of coffee to match that certain coffee-maker.

Why am I dwelling on coffee? Because it is a perfect example of how people on tight budgets or low incomes are losing money, actually hemorrhaging it, in fact, on things that cost far too much for the convenience they provide and they don't even realize it! Moreover, many, perhaps most, don't even realize the actual real costs involved to them. Again, you don't have to go without. You just have to choose a different way of going about whatever it is you think you must have, a cheaper, wiser way, and you will say a lot of money! Remember these rules:

RULE NUMBER ONE ABOUT MONEY OUTGO: Don't lie to yourself about how much you're spending. Look at it with a realistic eye. By doing that, you can then decide how and where to cut expenses. Think of the coffee example, of the costs of eating out, etc.

RULE NUMBER TWO ABOUT MONEY OUTGO: Don't try to claim it's a necessary treat and one you just can't do without. First, a "necessary treat" is an oxymoron. A treat is something special, not something normally needed. Moreover, nobody "needs" an overly high-priced cup of coffee every single day. They just want it. There is a big difference between want and need, and that difference is usually price, a high one!

They may "need" coffee, but as stated, they can get good quality at far cheaper prices. So again, look for a way to have that same treat, whatever it may be, but in a much cheaper and smarter way. Again, I'm not saying you have to do without. You just have to approach things in a cleverer way.

Do you want that extra-large pizza with everything on it? Buy it fresh at the supermarket and bake it at home. Even Walmart has them, deli fresh pizzas, and you can dress the pizza up a bit, if you like, customize it to your tastes, and then bake it. Toss in a few liters of soda to go with it, and even buy those cheesy breadsticks at the supermarket, if you want them. You will have the same meal, a fresh one, and so healthier for a fraction of the cost of those delivered pizzas or fast food stop-offs you make on the way home. Once more; you don't have to do without! You just have to be smart about how you go about things. And really, how hard is it to toss a self-rising pizza in the oven for a lousy fifteen minutes?

Nor am I picking on just a few items. This is an across-the-board thing you have to do. The average, individual-sized bottle of water, bought one at a time, is around $1 minimum these days in many stores, and even more in others. Check and see how many bottles of water you are drinking like this per week, per month, per year! It can come to hundreds or even thousands of dollars! Furthermore, many experts on the subject say that often plain tap water is just as good or better. Los Angeles City water, for instance, is said to rank better than several national brands of bottled water for purity and taste!

So do you really have to have that bought bottle of water every day, or several times a day? Can you really afford it? Do you need to afford it? If so, why? If your tap water isn't to your liking, it's far cheaper to buy a filter that goes on the tap rather than to pay repeatedly for bottled water!

I know one woman, "Sandy" who wanted to carry around a bottle of water all the time because it was "the in thing to do" and all her business associates were doing it. She wanted to "be part of the group," but really couldn't afford to spend that kind of money on water, water that per gallon was costing as much as a gallon of gasoline in some cases! So she would only occasionally buy a bottle of water and then refill it from her tap, which she had purchased a filter for. She then capped the bottle of water and took it to work with her. She would refill it whenever she needed to. Smart woman! She saved hundreds, if not thousands of dollars doing this! Not to mention, she helped the environment enormously by doing this.

So watch your outgo by watching what you spend your hard-earned money on. In addition, no, you don't have to have the discipline to keep a journal of your daily routine expenses, but you have to be aware of them, and you have to do something intelligent about them. To do this, attack each aspect of what you are spending money on, item by item, and see if there are not cheaper alternatives, or if you really need that item at all!

AGAIN, IF YOU WANT MORE MONEY, ONE OF THE MAIN WAYS OF ACHIEVING THIS GOAL IS BY SHRINKING YOUR OUTGOING COSTS! THIS IS THE SAME AS INCREASING YOUR INCOME FOR ALL PRACTICAL PURPOSES. IT GIVES YOU MORE MONEY TO SPEND ON OTHER THINGS, AS WITH THOSE BILLS YOU AREN'T PAYING ON TIME, OR SAY YOU CAN'T AFFORD TO PAY!

Learn to be more judicious about how much money you spend on things and where and when you spend it. For example, instead of eating out every other day, simply because it's "easier," try making dining out a real treat, as in once a week, or every couple of weeks, instead of as just another part of a "ho-hum" daily routine and even several times a day. You will probably enjoy dining out more that way, since anticipation of something that is more of a special event is part of the fun.

If you want to start making money right away by plugging those leaks in your outgo, here's a partial list of ways you can cut back without having to sacrifice those things you want.

Coffee/Tea/Water: As mentioned, make it at home. Use a good brand, one you really like for coffee or tea and then take it with you in a traveling cup. This won't take you any longer than standing in a line or at a drive-thru at some coffee chain retailer. Remember, over 30 years, the home brew comes to less than $1,000. The "store bought" is over $23,000. That's a heck of a savings and a nice savings nest egg. If the equivalent is banked each month, then allowed to earn interest, it comes to even more! The same holds for bottled water.

This is also true of many other places and food items, as well, even donuts! Do a little research. Don't be afraid to change your behavior pattern a bit, especially when it doesn't mean you have to sacrifice anything! What works for coffee in this case, works for just about any purchase like this you might make.

Eating Out: Eating out is downright expensive these days and there simply is no way around the fact. Yet, as of this year, and as mentioned earlier, Americans now spend more on eating out than they do on groceries! Therefore, if you want to save a LOT of money, curtail the practice of eating out so much and do good substitutes by buying "fast food" style foods if you like, but ones you can prepare at home quickly and easily, such as supermarket fresh pizzas, sandwiches (better yet, make your own), etc. In any case, you can still eat out occasionally, but make it more of an event, something that isn't every day, or every other day.

Phones Cost. There are many ways to cut down on phone costs. Try looking for different plans. DON'T include the cost of that expensive, state-of-the-art phone in any long-term contract (one, two, or more years) that you might decide to go with. You pay much more for the phone over the period of such a contract than it's worth that way, and you are then caught in a vicious cycle. About the time your phone contract ends, your phone is obsolete, and so you are "hooked" into buying a new one on yet another long-term, high-priced plan yet again. Again, it's a vicious cycle, and frankly, it's meant to be. This is how phone companies make their money, and again, that's at your expense! It's always at your expense! **FOR THEM TO MAKE MONEY, YOU LOSE MONEY! It's a direct transfer of wealth and not in the right direction!**

Televisions Services Cost. These can be as much as a power utility bill for television service, if one isn't careful. Furthermore, one can just as easily get "locked" into such bills with no easy way out, at least, not without paying a hefty price to do so. Avoid contracts that extend for one, two, or more years. The television provider industry is changing rapidly and you don't want to be locked into paying a high price for something for two years, when cheaper alternatives become available.

The average cost of cable television, and/or satellite television, has really soared in the last decade. What was once around $50 a month is now closer to $150, especially if you "bundle" your phone, internet, and television channels into one package. This comes to the same cost as my monthly electric bill.

In addition, there are hidden costs for these contracts in some instances, as well. For example, I found that bundled phone service with one cable company, who shall be nameless, after the first year, went from $19 a month to darn close to $50 a month! This was just for an internet based phone service and not the rest of it, not cable and internet. What did I do? I went online and purchased a month-to-month, Internet, phone service, one just as could as that cable company in quality, and for just $10 a month!

Are there alternatives to high-priced contracts with television providers? Of course, there are. Do a little research. It doesn't take a lot. I was paying close to $130 a month for satellite television. In the process, I was paying to get channels I wanted by having also to pay for a bunch of channels I didn't want! Moreover, there were far more of those in the package than ones I wanted to watch. Also, I was paying lease payments monthly for each extra receiver box I had (for bedrooms, etc.).

This was not a bundled service at the time, but just for television channels. I found an alternative that worked for me. I bought an outdoor, high resolution antenna for $90.00. Within a month, it had more than paid for itself in savings by not having to pay monthly fixed costs to the satellite provider. And, I had over fifty channels this way.

Since we are all paying for internet, don't overlook streaming devices or free services like YouTube, Pluto, and others. There are a lot of movies and shows on YouTube, and lots of great documentaries and other items, as well. Alternative ways to reduce costs for you are to substitute cable or satellite for such pay services as Amazon, Netflix and/or Hulu, etc. Even combined, the two are far, far less in cost than most standard cable fees are these days.

Electricity Costs: Here's a cost that seems just to keep slowly (sometimes, rapidly) going up with seemingly no real way to control it, but there are ways to do this, even so. Yes, we all know about yelling at the kids to turn lights off when they aren't using them, etc., but there are other, subtler and effective ways to make major changes in your monthly electricity costs.

At the very least, try having your bill "averaged" by the power company. Many power companies will do this. I do this, because I don't like being hit with unexpectedly high bills. By having the bill averaged, it guarantees that I pay the same amount each month, so I'm not smacked in the face with astronomically high bills at the peak of winter and/or summer, respectively. This makes paying other bills each month easier for you, since you don't have to worry about one month having the power bill double or triple on you because it's been too hot or too cold recently. If you happen to overpay this bill because you use less electricity, it is refunded to you once a year.

Light bulbs: Another and I must say excellent way of saving money is changing out those old incandescent light bulbs. With the fluorocarbon lights came out, I switched all the bulbs in my house to those. Yes, there was an initial cost, but my power company, Duke Energy, actually gave away boxes of such light bulbs at the time as an incentive to help save power. I jumped at the chance. Yes, I wasn't crazy about the quality of the light, a bit garish for my tastes, and nor did I like the fact it took several seconds for the lights to reach full brightness. However, these were minor considerations compared to savings in costs on my power bill. This more than persuaded me I had done the right thing.

Immediately, my power bill went down by no less than $50 a month. From $200 to $150 a month was a significant change for me. In addition, and besides using far less power to work, the new light bulbs lasted far longer than the incandescent ones did and this, too, was a savings.

Now, my power company is offering reduced prices on LED bulbs and despite my other ones still functioning well, I'm switching out once more, because LED uses VERY little electricity, even compared to the fluorocarbon bulbs, and they had another advantage: they come on at full strength immediately and with a better quality light, I feel. LED lights use so little electricity that they will run for days off batteries, as with the LED lights on Christmas trees. The advantages of such light bulbs are amazing, and the reduction in power bill costs cannot be underestimated. Moreover, the things have an amazingly long lifespan!

Another measure is to plug all your various appliances into power strips. This helps protect them against power surges, and more importantly, when you switch off the power strip, all the appliances, such as giant screen televisions, etc., are turned off completely. Many devices, in order to have the "instant on" features, have power running to them all the time. One way to stop this power consumption is to use power strips. **Always remember; money not going out, is extra money you can use for other purposes! It becomes more disposable income.**

There are other ways to save on outgo, as well, and sometimes, as with the Internet streaming boxes, they might require an initial investment, but usually one that returns to you in the form of big savings and often very quickly. For example, when it comes time to get another car, quit buying your "dream vehicle" which is a short-lived dream in any case, because most of us change our cars every few years. Instead, buy an efficient and economical one.

In addition, no, I don't want to hear how your family (usually four people or less these days) needs a big vehicle! If you do, feel you absolutely have to have one, go for a hybrid SUV or pickup.

Preferably, go for more of a compact hybrid car. I did this and the savings, whether gasoline prices are up or down, are enormous! For all practical purposes, my gasoline costs per month are inconsequential! This was so when gas was $4 a gallon, and it is still now at $2.28 a gallon. Hybrids save money! A lot of it! I imagine electric cars do, too, although I haven't owned one of those. For me, their range before needing recharging is still insufficient for my purposes. Still, hybrids work and work well. They are cheap to use, much cheaper to buy these days, and they will save you money while helping the environment.

Heating and Cooling. My advice, if you don't already have one, is to get a good programmable thermostat for you heating system. They are easy to install (I did it, so they must be easy!). The price for these thermostats is usually just above or below $100.

By programming your heating and/or cooling for different times of the day (mine has four cycles, but also other options, such as "every day," "weekends," etc.), you will say a lot of money! Once set, such thermostats do far more to control energy costs than you manually upping and downing the thermostat randomly and every day, even several times a day.

Why? Well, first, the programmable type of thermostat often has a feature, where as a cycle comes to a close and the next one begins, if there is a noticeable difference in temperature settings (being higher for the next cycle), as for heating, the thermostat slowly begins raising the heat a few minutes ahead of time. I have a heat pump and this means the auxiliary heating strip, a power consuming pig of a thing, isn't activated to jump the heat up at all once this way. This saves money!

Having set temperatures that aren't constantly being raised and lowered all the time saves money! Moreover, try shaving off just one or two degrees on the heating or cooling side, and you will be amazed how much more money that saves you in electricity costs over the month.

This method does not deprive you of any comforts, but having a thermostat set to automatic means less changing of temperatures and less often. You can still manually up the temperature a few degrees if at any time, you are too cool or warm, but at the end of that cycle, the thermostat reverts to the preset temperatures. So if you are cold in the evening and raise the temperature some, it doesn't mean it will stay higher all night, and long after you are snug and warm in your bed it will drop again, even if you forget to set it down.

Gardening: For a long time, I was "too busy" to do my own lawn care, so I hired a gardening service to mow my lawn every ten days. Then one day, I realized that being "too busy" meant just spending a lot more time watching more TV. I resolved this wasn't a good thing. So I let the gardener go and did my own mowing.

Within a matter of months, the savings were enough for me to purchase outright, a ride-on lawn mower, and the job became a snap! (I have almost two acres, of which about an acre needs mowing.) Granted, I still hate weeding and will use the gardener once every few months to do that, but even so, I have saved a lot of money by doing the mowing and edging jobs myself. And truthfully, it's a 40-minute job, and no big deal. Furthermore, instead of being a couch potato, I was more active. By the way, did you know that statistically, people who do some gardening, live longer lives on average than people who don't? Worth considering.

Transportation Costs. We already mentioned how possibly to save on gasoline consumption costs by buying smaller vehicles and/or hybrid ones. There are other ways to reduce costs, as well. Have less than two miles to get to work? Then WALK! It saves wear and tear on your vehicle, gas, and/or bus, train, subway, or taxi fees, and it's very healthy. I'm no longer young and I walk a brisk two miles every day. Walking to and from work is a great way to get healthy, stay healthy, and save a lot of money! This improves your lifestyle, and does not detract from it in any way. Moreover, again, you are helping the environment.

Furthermore, you will be amazed at how much better you feel after just several weeks of doing this. Walking and bicycling are good forms of exercise, so not only are you saving money, but you are improving your health.

There are other ways to reduce transportation costs, as well. These include bicycling, but also carpooling, and more. Be creative; use one of these methods and save money, and develop a healthier lifestyle into the bargain!

Housing Costs:

For those dedicated to the idea or really reducing their outgo, using all of the methods already mentioned is a good way to start. Even just using some of them is of tremendous value. Remember that cup of coffee a day I keep harping about? Just keep saying to yourself: "$23,000!" Need a nest egg when you retire? Do you want a trip around the world in your later years? There is the money for it right there! Furthermore, if you bank the equivalent savings each month, again, interest is added to it, so your final nest egg will be considerably more than just $23,000! It should end up being closer to $130,000, depending on interest rates over the long haul.

Earlier, I mentioned we would talk more about home mortgages. Well, housing costs can be a big part of one's monthly outgo. In many cases, it might even probably be your biggest single expense. And changing this for the better is one of the more difficult things to do, since we all need a place to live for ourselves and our families. However, there are things you can do.

As I mention repeatedly in this book, and just as with other expenses, you must first take stock of your housing situation and housing costs. Only then can you make adjustments. And believe it or not, you always can, although sometimes it can mean some sacrifice.

Some questions:

Do you rent a house or an apartment?

Do you own a home with an outstanding mortgage?

Do you live alone, but in a place with more than one bedroom, possibly?

In the case of renting a house or an apartment, you can look for alternative arrangements. Maybe, if you are willing to have a slightly longer commute time, you can move to an area further from your place of employment (out of the city?) and so achieve a cheaper rent. You might even get more bang from your buck this way and live in a cleaner environment, one well away from city pollution.

I live about 20 minutes from the nearest large city, and the difference in home prices and rental costs is great. A small house that would rent for over a $2,000 downtown, rents for around $700 in my area. It does mean a further commute, but the freeway is close by and that helps.

In the case of owning a home, that's a tougher, but not an insoluble problem to reduce your costs. If you mortgage includes your taxes and insurance, check with your insurance company for ways to reduce the costs of your insurance. I did this at one time and was able substantially to reduce these costs. This resulted in a lower monthly mortgage payment because the escrow fees (included in my mortgage), were then lower.

I found I had been over insured for years! Taxes might work the same way, if you are lucky. Some states give those with a small income a reduced rate on their taxes. Homesteading in some states, helps reduce tax costs. And for those who are of a "certain age," often they can get some tax relief, as well, due to their age. All this varies from state to state, so you have to do a little research in that regard.

Your House as Money. Your home is an expensive proposition, but it can work for you, help you to make money How? Well, there are a number of ways:

Roommates. Having financial problems, but have a spare room or rooms? Whether a home or an apartment, you have a means of making more money if you have such a room. Rent them out! There are lots of websites where you can post for free that you have a room for rent. If you don't have an available room, are using it as a study or something, think about combining your master bedroom with your study. Usually, there is room for a desk, chair, and computer, along with a filing cabinet or two without overfilling your master bedroom. That will then leave the other room empty and ready to use as a rentable spare bedroom.

You can save a lot of money by finding a roommate you are compatible with and there are lots of other benefits besides. You have company if you live alone, someone else there in case of an emergency. Their rent money helps defray the cost of your mortgage and your utilities or if you have two roommates (two spare bedrooms), then it might just pay for all of that!

Caveat:

Of course, finding a compatible roommate isn't always easy, and many people are scared off of doing this for this very reason. Don't be afraid. You can meet with prospective roommates, have a long chat with them, vet them, and see for yourself if they are compatible people to live with you. Roommates in most states are not considered the same as renting an apartment to someone. The law tends to recognize that a roommate falls into a different category precisely because they do live with you in your own home. So check out the laws on this for your state. In my state, the law does recognize that having someone in your home living with you is different from renting some type of rental unit to them, and so the law is more lenient for you, as a landlord, often in this regard. Again, it is more lenient in this regard in my state. Check out yours.

Some Things To Consider For Selecting Roommates:

1. If you like your privacy, make sure the person you are considering renting to has a fulltime job. This way, they'll be gone for at least forty or so hours a week giving you lots of private time for yourself. Make sure, though, that their hours are such that they are compatible with your living style. You don't necessarily want someone who sleeps all day (or is roaming around the house all day) and then leaves at night for work just when you are ready to go to bed. Not much in the way of private time under those conditions!

2. Run a credit check (with their permission) to see if they have a good or bad credit rating. This will let you know if they will pay their rent to you on time. However, keep in mind that many possibly good roommates may have lousy credit. The reason they are looking to rent a room is because often they can't pass the more stringent tests required by many apartment rental agencies.

3. Make sure the person doesn't use drugs/alcohol. If they do use alcohol, at least be certain the person does not drink to excess. I had a problem with this once and had to ask the person to leave, ultimately. People who can't control their drinking or use drugs can be disagreeable and even violent, and often can cause damage, intentionally or unintentionally to your home. Make it clear you will not tolerate such behavior before you rent to such people, and make it clear you will ask them to leave immediately if they do. In some states, you can rent a room under that state's hotel/motel law, which allows you to evict them in just hours. Check with an attorney on this matter.

4. Make sure that the rental agreement only allows for the one individual and not others besides. Also, specify if you allow them to have visitors at all, overnight visitors, etc. You don't want an endless parade of total strangers, for example, coming and going at all hours. My advice is to seek a legal rental agreement through an attorney (they aren't expensive), or download one from a legal service online. Better to be safe than sorry and a little investment in such a legal lease is always a good idea, as any attorney will tell you.

5. Consider how long the prospective roommate is likely to stay. For example, no matter what a college student may tell you, they will probably only want the room for the school year at most and much more probably, only for the semester. In that time, being young, they can often cause damages and disobey rules. So consider carefully before renting to students.

6. Talk to the person. Get to know them a little. You might want to know, for instance, if they are neat-freaks, or sloppy in nature, and then decide if that is compatible with how you are. In other words, simply consider all the dos and don'ts of what you want in a roommate. Take your time and pick a person that seems most compatible with you and your lifestyle.

Again, different states approach what you can and can't consider in such matters of choosing a roommate with regard to discriminatory practices, so make sure you follow the laws in this, but once more, most states treat roommates as a different category than actual renters of a separate property. They do this, because they know the living arrangements are much more intimate than just renting someone a separate house or apartment.

My personal advice is to always have a rental agreement, and always have the rules included in the rental agreement, and make sure the roommate signs them as having been read, understood, and that they acknowledge they will conform to them. That way, they can't claim to have not known what was expected of them later.

I'm no attorney and therefore I can't give any legal advice here, so if you need legal advice to draw up such a rental agreement or have questions answered, contact an attorney of your choice, or use a reputable online legal service to accomplish this task. Once more, the money spent is well worth it for your protection, to make sure you are covered, and that you aren't in some way accidentally breaking the law or being discriminatory. Also, it is advisable to check with your home insurance company to see what is or is not covered under such a situation.

Upside Down Homes. Now we come to those who bought their homes at the peak of the market bubble prices and still owe more than the home is worth. Often, these people have high monthly mortgages, as well. I have friends in Florida who were paying over $3,500 a month on their mortgage. When the economy nosedived, so did their business income. And sadly, we are in just such hard times once more due to the pandemic. With regard to my friends, they ended up having to walk away from the retirement home of their dreams. They let it go into foreclosure.

If you are in this predicament, you will seriously have to consider if this might not be best for you, as well. To pay for years to come on a house that just is no longer worth anywhere near what you paid for it is a terribly hard thing to do, and I don't recommend taking this step lightly. You must consider all your other options first!

However, sometimes, you just have to get that "monkey off your back," and so be able to start life afresh. You might be paying a huge monthly mortgage, when if you walked away from it, declared bankruptcy if necessary, you could then purchase or rent the equivalent home for far less.

Another way to go is to try to negotiate with your bank, to see if you can reduce the mortgage or be granted some type of other relief with regard to your debt. Again, seeking the advice of legal counsel is always a good idea and the cost is minimal, especially when compared to the costs of continuing to pay a huge mortgage on a home that is just not worth that value anymore.

The important thing here is not to feel trapped, because you are not! Only you can trap you! Only you can free yourself! You have free will and I know many people who just had to get out from under their massive debt burdens caused by the last economic crash. The same is already happening with this economic depression, which is pandemic induced.

They did this by declaring bankruptcy, just walking away from their overpriced and costly homes. It's wrenching for many to have to do this, because of feelings of having failed or being ashamed, but there is often also a great relief, as the worry of meeting that massive mortgage when they've lost their jobs is then over for good and finally off their shoulders. This year (2020) major corporations by the dozen are also doing just that, declaring bankruptcy and at a higher rate than we have seen in the better part of a century. If they can do it, so can you!

Again, this is a big step, a truly major one, and you should consider carefully if you have any other options that might work instead. Perhaps refinancing the home, getting the mortgage company/bank to reconsider the amount of the loan, or the cost of the monthly payments, etc. Only if these approaches should fail, or simply aren't viable for you, should you take the extreme step of just letting the house go.

Yet, not only will you have tremendous relief if you get out from under such an intolerable burden, but you will then be able to use at least a portion of what you were paying in monthly mortgage for something else, like starting your own business. Moreover, there are people with not only one, but two or more mortgages on their house. This is often an untenable situation for the homeowners, especially if their jobs have been lost or changed due to the Great Recession and now the Depression into a lower paying one.

My personal opinion, for what it's worth in such instances, is that just walking away may be the best way to go. Again, each person must make this decision for themselves, and only after having explored other options first, and seeking the advice of an authorized expert or lawyer about the matter. I stress that point here.

Yet, having been a real estate broker, I'm all too aware many people have no other option, and the struggle to meet exorbitant monthly housing payments when having lost their jobs was sometimes literally killing them with stress and worry, and even physically, because of often having to work two or more jobs to make ends meet! For me, that's just not worth it!

In any case, give your housing situation some careful thought and then make whatever decisions you personally feel you need to, in order to improve your financial situation. As for my friends in Florida, they have another home now, one they can afford. They have since had it renovated, and they are very happy! So life does go on, and if you work it right, possibly for the better!

There are other ways to save money on a monthly basis. This can be by buying the store brands (generic) of many grocery and pharmaceutical items, rather than name brands, for instance. Also, what about growing a vegetable/fruit garden? Organically grown fruits and vegetables are all the rage, and far cheaper to grow yourself than to buy. Organic vegetables come at a real premium to purchase! Not only that, but if you have children, it's a great way to teach them about growing things, the magic of making plants mature and bear edible items.

There are many other ways to save money, as well. Use your imagination. Get creative. Find ways to do things better and cheaper, and more efficiently. At the risk of using a tired cliché, "think outside of the box." Roommates are one way to go, I once used this method to advantage. If you have two cars and seldom use one of them, get rid of it! Sell it and pay it off if there is still a loan on it. You save that monthly loan cost, insurance, maintenance fees, and registration fees by doing so. If you live close to work, consider walking or using a bicycle. You will save on gas and perhaps make the environment a little better for your efforts.

Remember; you don't have to deprive yourself; you just need to seek good alternatives that cost less. Reorder your thinking a bit, change your priorities as to what's important in your life. Then find some way to keep those things you want, but to do it more cheaply. You will be surprised at just how much you can save with this sort of a can-do attitude.

REMEMBER, WHAT YOU DON'T SPEND EACH MONTH IS MONEY IN YOUR POCKET AT THE END OF THE MONTH TO DO WITH AS YOU WISH! IT IS A WAY OF INCREASING YOU INCOME BY DECREASING YOUR OUTGO! IN JUST A FEW WEEKS' TIME, YOU CAN INCREASE YOUR INCOME BY DECREASING WHAT YOU SPEND EACH MONTH!

You know the old saying, "it takes money to make money." It does, and one fast way to get that money is to decrease your outgo! So make a game of it. Try to figure out how to economize, to cut outgo without overly depriving yourselves or changing your lifestyles into impossibly severe ones. Again, make a game of it. Because in the finally analysis, moneymaking is a sort of game we all have to play. So we might as well get good at it! We might as well learn to enjoy it. And you will be surprised at what a feeling of satisfaction you get from achieving savings by using these methods of cutting your outgo.

The title of the next chapter is a bit misleading, because, in fact, if you follow the steps on cutting your outgo, you already have started to increase your income. However, just decreasing your outgo, although very helpful, often isn't enough. This is especially so, if you have an overall income that is low to begin with. For many people, this is all too real a problem these days. For those who have lost well-paying jobs, have had to resort to taking poor paying ones, it can be a real trial to meet existing and fixed expenses.

Still, you will see how to start actually increasing your overall income if you follow the steps outlined in the next chapters. You can do this. Anyone can, and the marvelous thing is that there are just so many ways of accomplishing this. So many ways, in fact, that this step has to be broken up into a number of parts.

Don't worry. This is a good thing, because it means you will have many alternatives as to exactly how you increase your income. Since this is a lengthy subject, again, I am dividing it into several parts. These include assessing your current possibilities for income, your options, and how you can increase actually increase that income.

CHAPTER FIVE

Credit Card Debt — Snowball
And Debt Avalanche Methods

This type of debt is a big one for many people. It was for me. As we struggle to make ends meet, we often end up using credit cards or perhaps even personal loans as a stopgap measure, fully intending to pay it off each month, but somehow never quite managing to do so. That means that as the months go by, the debt on those credit cards keeps going up.

Unfortunately, although often seeming to be necessary when struggling to meet payments on time, it is a bit like a drug addiction. With large interest rates on those credit cards, along with the cost of all those charges you make on them, you only go deeper and more quickly into debt. Credit cards may help you meet your financial obligations for a while, but in the long run, they only make matters worse! Therefore, not only do we have other debts we can't meet, but all too often, we have that added burden of a heavy credit card debt, as well.

Now, we've already talked about saving money by decreasing your outgo, how that quickly begins adding money to your income by doing so, since it isn't going out like water through a sieve to all sorts of incidentals. But what to do with those savings?

Let's be honest here, just saving by not spending on all those exorbitantly priced cups of coffee, lunches out, etc., is not enough to balance the sheets. Although you are now saving money by not spending it unnecessarily, you haven't reduced your debt burden...yet.

There are two main ways to go about doing this, of paying down credit card debt and various types of loans These are:

The Snowball Method and Debt Avalanche Method. First, we will concentrate on the **Snowball Debt Method.** This is the one I used and it worked well for me, very well! Moreover, this isn't just for credit card debt but can be used for any combination of debts. Whether student loans, car loans, mortgages, medical loans, or even those terribly expensive payday loans, etc., this does work and work well!

The trick here is to pay off the smallest debt first. Use those savings you have now made by cutting monthly expenses to pay down on the smallest debt you have. Now, this may not seem wise. After all, the smallest debt may have a low rate of interest, whereas a larger debt might have a much higher rate of interest. So wouldn't it be better to pay that larger one off first? Some people think so and this is why there is the other method, the **Avalanche Method**, as well. However, I personally favor (because it worked so well for me) the **Snowball Method** to pay off my debts, so that I could get rid of some of them much sooner than by using the other method.

So, what you do is:

1. Add the extra money you saved from cutting your monthly expenses by using it to pay down the smallest debt you have. Anything extra in the way of available cash you get, add to that debt payment whenever you can, as well. I mean this! Use any windfalls of money, tax refunds, etc., to increase and speed up this process of paying down that smallest debt. In the meantime, just pay the absolute minimum amount you are allowed to pay on your other debts. Just Concentrate on getting rid of that smallest one first.

2. Once you've paid off that smallest debt, take the payments you were making on that one, which you now no longer have to make because you've paid it off, and pay down the next smallest loan. If possible, and really try to do this, on that next loan, make the minimum payment you've been making already, PLUS the money you would have been paying on that first loan/debt you have now paid off. For example, if you were paying $45 minimum payment on a second credit card, and just paid off the first one, then take the payment money saved from having gotten rid of that first card's debt, add it to the $45 minimum on the second card's debt and keep the process going.

3. Once you have started this process, keep it up! Keep attacking the next lowest debt, (the one closest to being paid off already) in that order. Always take all the money you were paying on the first, second, and third debts you paid off, and then apply it all to the next to pay that off, and so on.

Now, you aren't doing this in the order of the ones with the highest interest rates first, but rather the ones that are the smallest amount of debt and so quickest to be able to pay off, instead. This approach keeps releasing more and more money, more swiftly, and so adds to the money you can then apply to the remaining loan payments.

This works! It has the advantage of allowing you to quickly see you are making headway, that you are removing that burden of debt that's been hanging over you, and gives you hope. It is the more positive-feeling one of the two approaches, I think. Yes, it isn't mathematically the one that gives you the most savings over the long haul, but when you are in a desperate situation, it is probably going to be the quickest method for you to begin to see positive results, to quickly lighten your debt burden.

At one point in my life, I had close to $62,000 in debts, not counting my mortgage. I had over $50,000 in credit card debt, and a car payment of $500 a month, as well. This wasn't counting any utility bills or other incidental costs either. That was a lot of money at the time. Still is, I feel. I was being buried alive in debt. I was a real estate agent at the time and the real estate market wasn't very good. All I could manage was to try to make the minimum payments on all those credit cards and very little more.

Then the worst happened. Under the second President Bush, a bill was passed by the House and Senate that upped how much in the way of a minimum payment had to be paid on such credit card debts. The intention of the bill was good, to allow people, by making the new and higher payment, to actually, eventually pay off the credit card debt. Up until then, the minimum was lower, to the point where all one was doing was just servicing the debt, but making no headway in paying it off! So yes, the intention was good.

However, for me, it spelled disaster! Suddenly, the minimum payments on all my credit cards went up! Where before I was just managing to meet my obligations, now I was in trouble, real trouble of falling behind. I was frantic. I thought of a debt consolidation loan—don't do those, is my advice. They only extend the lifetime of your debt even longer, and any monthly savings you get by lowering that monthly payment with a consolidation loan are apt to simply vanish somehow, leaving you really no better off. So a debt consolidation loan was out of the question for me. I thought of a personal loan, but at fairly high interest rates, it wouldn't help much.

Truth to tell, I very much doubted that at the time I would have even qualified for such loans, so heavy was my debt burden already. So I had to try something else. I started by reducing my monthly expenses, exactly as described earlier. I had to! I had to do something!

Then, I had to figure out how to approach paying down my debt. I figured I was about three months from going under, of being late in my payments, so I had to act quickly. Then, luckily for me, I managed to sell a property as an agent. My share of the commission was a wonderful (to me at the time, at least), $12,000!

A friend argued I should pay down the credit card debt with the highest interest rate first (a whopping 32 percent!). It was also my biggest single debt, of some $16,000. However, the $12,000 commission I had made simply wouldn't pay it all off. It wasn't enough. It would still leave $4,000 at the higher interest rate level and also a fairly high minimum monthly payment, as well, and so not really of much help overall, other than a bit of a reduction in cost on a monthly payment on that one card.

Again, so not much help to me really, not for investing the whole $12,000 in that approach. I decided to go with the Snowball Method. Although at the time, I didn't know there was a name for such a thing. I argued with my friend that it would be better to pay something off in its entirety, and so release myself from that burden immediately, and thus, then allowing me to take some of that saved money to add to paying off my other debts.

I decided to pay off my car. It had about $12,500 owing on it, and the payments, as mentioned, were $500 a month. None of my credit card minimums were near that amount, most being somewhere between $100 and $300 a month. So I paid off the remaining amount due on the car, thus saving have to pay monthly on it for many more months.

I then took the money I had been paying on the car ($500 a month), and added it to the minimum payment I'd been paying on a credit card with the next lowest balance, and paid that down very quickly, in about five months and those were still tough times, very touch and go for me as to whether I could make all my payments. Remember, I couldn't meet all my obligations at the outset, so although my debt burden had gone down some, it was still high!

Again, that credit card was paid off in about five months. In the meantime, I had only been making the minimum payments on everything else. Even so, now, I could see a bit of light at the end of the tunnel. My income was finally a little more than equal to my debt outgo. What's more, I was enjoying getting out of debt! It became a real "thing," a sort of game for me to see the amounts on those cards drop and drop quickly!

So I just kept at it, kept pushing to pay off my debts one by one, and always the next lowest debt first. And believe me, when I paid off that credit card with the 32 percent interest rate (raised from 14 percent because I had been a week late with just one payment on it in 8 years!), you can only imagine my satisfaction! I immediately cancelled that card. Yes, I know it slightly and adversely affects your credit rating to cancel credit cards, but oh, there was such satisfaction in telling them to shove it! I loved it when they asked me why I was cancelling, and did I ever enjoy telling them! Yes, there is great satisfaction and it comes quickly with the **Snowball Method**.

By the way, in just 18 months, I was debt free. I had gone from sinking, floundering in a sea or flood of debt to saving my credit rating (actually improving it a great deal in the process), and becoming debt free, except for my mortgage payment. Truly, it was a great relief, and you can have that same relief, too! It might take longer depending on your circumstances and amount of debt, or perhaps less time, if your debt burden is less than mine was, but it works!

I'm a big fan of the **Snowball Method** for that reason. For me, personally, it was a lifesaver. It was only much later I found out that it was an actual method in financing to pay off debt. I had simply figured it out for myself. And of course, the reason it is called the **Snowball Method** is because your debt reduction snowballs by adding ever larger payments to remaining debts.

The Avalanche Method. This method is similar to the **Snowball Method** in that you make the minimum payments on all your debts, except one, the one with the largest or highest interest rate. You attack the debt by paying it down as quickly as you can with any extra money you might have (supposedly saved from making just minimum payments on all the other debts you have, but in my case, I was already doing that!). Once you have paid that debt off, you then go after the next one with the next largest interest rate.

The advantages of this method are that you really do save money by knocking out those high interest debts first. However, it takes quite a while for this method to show visible results. Most of us are not so mathematically oriented that we can enjoy the idea of simply reducing a massive debt in interest burden bit by bit, while still retaining all the other debt, as well. At least, I could not. I needed to see results, and fairly quickly! Most of us do. Such positive results give us the incentive to continue with our debt removal plan because we see actual results fairly soon on. However, the Avalanche Method does save you more money in the long run by reducing the high-interest credit card or household debts first.

Both methods work, but from what I've researched, more people seem to prefer the Snowball Method, as did I. I needed to see progress and fast. Most do. It helps to keep one going with the plan, just as going on a diet that shows steady weight loss helps a person to stick to that diet.

Truly, I was at the point of giving up and just declaring bankruptcy, which of course, would destroy my credit rating for years to come. I was just three months at most, away from having to do so when I started my **Snowball Method** plan.

Again, both methods work and they each have their positive and negatives. The choice is up to you. If you can manage to hang in there longer, the **Avalanche Method** is probably the best approach because overall, it saves you the most money. However, if you are the type who needs to see some sort of light at the end of the tunnel as quickly as possible, as did I, then the **Snowball Method** is probably the better way to go. I have to tell you; having more money each month to pay down on my remaining debts really made me breathe a lot easier! What a relief it was! But the choice of methods is yours, whichever works better for you.

By the way either method works and both are good. Moreover, they don't just work for credit card debt, either. I used the **Snowball Method** on a Personal Loan, paying more than I had to each month, in fact, any money I came up with during the month I would add to the payments, sometimes paying some money several times in one month toward the same debt. So yes, the methods work for almost all sorts of debts.

Another way to quickly reduce burdensome interest costs, which raise monthly loan payments, is if you can transfer your credit card debt to another credit card, or even get a personal loan. Often, you are granted a year or so without interest on such transfers to another credit card. This means that during that time, everything you pay on the debt is going to lower the debt itself and not just go to servicing the interest charges. This means you can pay the debt off more quickly. Be wary, though, of this approach. At the end of the year, the interest rate will go back on the remaining debt and it could even be higher than it was on the other credit card!

Moreover, be careful for another reason. There are usually transaction fees which can take away some of the benefits of doing such transfers.

Personal loans often have lower interest rates than credit cards, so to get one of those to pay off such cards could help you meet payment obligations, which on a monthly basis, hopefully, would then be lower. And you would be paying less overall because of that lower interest rate.

However, remember, if you are using a personal loan to accomplish this, there will still be interest charges, although usually not as high as credit cards charge. But DON'T stretch the loan out over a longer duration! That just means you will be paying longer, thus be in debt longer, then you would be otherwise.

CHAPTER SIX

The Fifth Step — Part One —
Increasing Your Income

When most of us think about increasing our income, one of the first things that comes to mind is the idea of getting a second job. When I once needed extra money, I went this route. I had been working at one law firm as an assistant there and found a second job three floors up in the same high-rise at another law firm. This was convenient. Both were considered fulltime jobs, but because one was night shift, I only had to work seven hours each day, rather than the usual eight.

Not wanting my good credit rating to suffer, I took the job because I needed to pay off debts. I figured that I could do this in less than a year. Wrong! To be honest with you, I don't know where the extra money was going (besides increased income taxes, etc.), but I was making little progress toward my goal. Oh, I met all my monthly obligations, but there seemed little extra besides and this despite what was considered to be two fulltime jobs! I realized the "temporary" job was fast becoming an extra and permanent one because of this fact. The problem was, I couldn't figure out why this was so, until I read an interesting article.

It seems that at the time, the average American, reasonably wealthy or not, only managed to save about seven percent of their total net income. This was true no matter what the income level was for each individual, except of course, for the very rich. But for most on average, it was just seven percent. For those earning millions every year, that was still a large amount of money! For those like me, just earning standard wages, the savings were thus almost negligible.

This situation has not improved. During the Great Recession, Americans on average only saved four percent of their income, or less. This has changed some during the Depression now going on, with most Americans saving more precisely because their normal means of spending it have been cut off. If one can't go to movies because of the pandemic, or plays, or concerts, or safely eat out, then one saves money. In short, they are increasing their income and saving it, by reducing their outgo! But without being able to work, that doesn't last for very long before they have to start using those extra savings.

In other words, they have automatically, liking it or not, have had to decrease their outgo, so it has increased their income accordingly. That extra money has been going in the bank…so far. Also, there is the added incentive for many Americans to save because they are fearful these days of the depression might worsen, so they are finally being more frugal and putting money aside in case of emergencies. Even so, most Americans have less than $1,000 in savings! These days, as I think we all know, that measly sum can be wiped out with just one minor expense, like a simple car repair, for example.

And whether or not by the time you may read this book we are still in a depression doesn't matter. The principles still apply, pandemic or no pandemic, depression or no depression. The principles still work!

Having trouble saving money is not a problem for the top ten percent and one percent. They make so much money, they simply can't spend it all. They have reached the point where for some, even if they spent a million dollars a day, they are making more money even than that daily. Such is the life of billionaires, one supposes, but it means that whether we "regular folk" like it or not, their wealth has reached the point of takeoff, where it grows by leaps and bounds, and so accordingly, does their savings.

On an episode of the documentary series, *Through The Wormhole*, starring Morgan Freeman, this fact was pointed out in no uncertain terms. Studies have shown that the very wealthy, the top one percent, actually don't even financially function in the same economy as the rest of us, but a different one more or less of their own devising. This "other" economy is one they control because money means power, and they use that power to influence politicians to pass laws and regulations more favorable to them making even more money. This is according to *Through The Wormhole*. The chart below clearly shows this:

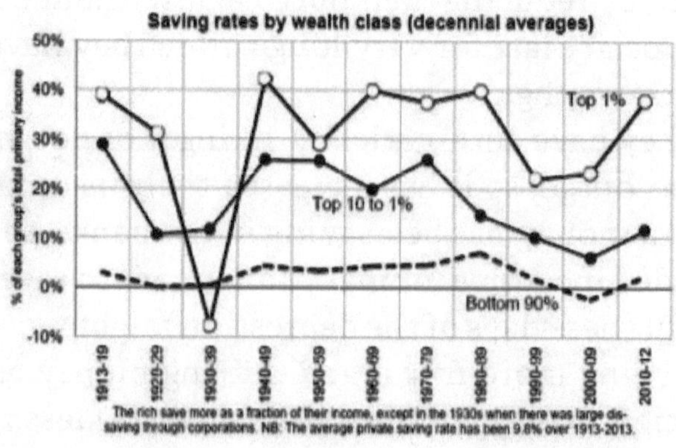

Source: Emmanuel Saez and Gabriel Zucman, *The Distribution of U.S. Wealth, Capital*

Please See References For A Link To Site For This Chart.

You can clearly see that the "bottom 90 percent" (us) often can't save any money, or can only save a small percentage of our income at best. While at the top, in the one percent bracket, they can save as much as 40 percent and in some years, even more. And this is with still enjoying a lavish daily lifestyle.

What's my point here? Well, *getting a second job may or may not mean a real net increase in your income versus your outgo!* Unfortunately, it seems to be the rule that as one expands their income, their outgo (somehow) goes up proportionately. The long-term rule is that for most of us, the 90 percent, regardless of our standard income levels, we only manage to normally save about 7 percent. That's whether one has one, two, or more jobs!

Therefore, if your idea of increasing your income is to work two jobs, you must be very careful of this fact! You must set up rules for yourself and your family that this extra money is untouchable, that it is only going to be used to pay off debts or to invest in some business idea that will make you even more money.

However, good luck with even that approach. Families have a way of suddenly needing money for more things when there is suddenly more income, such as dental work, clothing, extra-curricular activities, new appliances that one has put off buying, home repairs or improvements, and an extra or new car, etc. So keeping that extra income just for existing debts or to save for a future business, and not having it trickle away for newly created "needs" is no easy task! It is a very tricky thing to do, indeed! Again, the rules must be strict and strictly adhered to in order for the second job to act as real extra income to pay off existing debts or to be saved for a new business.

Caveat for Second Jobs: As mentioned above, if the income from second jobs is not used for paying off existing debts or a fund for a new business, the job then tends to become permanent with no great benefits long-term because the person's outgo climbs to meet their new income level, minus about 4 to 7 percent (currently). Moreover, burnout from working two jobs is a real problem, as well.

After just two to three months, the average person starts to suffer from physical, emotional, and mental stress trying to maintain the pace and meet all the demands now placed upon them. A second job should be for a definite timespan and be used for a specific purpose, to pay off existing debt, or to help you acquire another and better way to increase your income more permanently. There should be a start date and an end date for the second job. One has to see a light at the end of the tunnel to give them incentive to keep going and not simply feel trapped forever in an even worse situation than they had before!

Having given this warning, there are many types of second jobs one can do, including some from home, depending on one's personal abilities and preferences. Here are just some examples:

Freelancing: If you have any skills that you can use to freelance, e.g., writing, accounting, editing, copywriting, computer programming, IT, consulting of any sort, etc., freelancing is a good way to go. Many sites on the Internet allow different types of freelancers to meet up with clients. Clients list their jobs and freelancers can then bid on them. The best bid gets the job, although this sometimes is a higher bid, because the particular freelancer is the best qualified of that bid group.

Such websites also often act as the escrow holder of the monies, making the client deposit the full amount and holding it until you, the freelancer, have met certain "milestones" along the way, when some of the funds are released, and/or until the job is finished.

If there are problems, such sites can also act as arbitrators. You do get an IRS tax form 1099 Misc. for this work, usually, unless it is an out-of-country client, in which case you are responsible for reporting that income to the IRS yourself.

Caveat: A caveat here for writing-style jobs. Beware of which bidding sites you use. Some cater to third-world freelancers. These often bid very low prices for work compared to western-industrial freelancers, and so make it hard to compete. The upside is that many of these people are not native English speakers and more often than not, the job will list this necessity "must be native English speaking." In any case, choose the site that best fits your abilities and monetary income requirements. Do remember, there are freelance sites for many types of work, as well, not just for writing. Again, whether you are a graphic designer, programmer, IT professional, or whatever, there is almost certainly a site you can go to and use.

Virtual Assistant: This can be a great second job and it applies to a lot of different types of work. Also, you can find such jobs on the freelance-style websites, as well. Basically, a virtual assistant is literally that; you handle being an assistant to some firm or employer via the Internet, working from your home or wherever you have access to the Internet. There are many types of companies looking for virtual assistants. Everything from building contractors, lawyers, publications, to…well just about anybody. Usually, no more than a high school diploma is needed and the tasks you do will vary for whoever is hiring you. It may involve scheduling their appointments for them, fact checking, typing up various types of documents, etc. Average pay for this can be quite variable, so check out a number of job requests to get an idea of what you think you are worth for any particular type of assistant. This is a fast growing field.

Medical Transcriber: There is good money in this, as well. The task involves transcribing doctors/specialists notes into readable medical reports. Currently, the average wage for this is about $17.00 an hour.

Lawn And Yard Maintenance: This is not a great paying second job, but it is in high demand and the hours are often quite flexible. Often, you can use the owner's tools, so investment in buying your own equipment isn't an absolute necessity. Also, this work tends to be seasonal, depending on the region of the country you are living in. Average wage for this is around $14.00 an hour, but in some areas, higher. Demand for such workers is growing.

Customer Service (at home): This might be a good job if you like dealing with people. Usually, it is answering the phone during set hours, and these are usually evening, night, or early morning. For many people, this makes customer service work ideal, because it fits with the schedule of their existing jobs. The average pay is approximately $17.00 an hour as of the publishing of this book, and of course, is subject to change. The demand for this type of work is growing as many customer service departments are now no longer outsourcing such work to other countries, and because of the recent pandemic, have moved customer services to employees who stay in their own homes.

Chauffeuring/Bus Driver: The demand for school bus drivers is high, as well as for other types of bus drivers, for large and small buses (senior courtesy buses, etc.) Often this requires you to have a "chauffeur" class driver's license, but these are not hard to obtain in most states. Average wage: $20.00 an hour. There is a good demand for such drivers and it is growing.

All these jobs allow you a great deal of freedom, time flexibility, and do not have anyone "looking over your shoulder" while you work, so they can be ideal second jobs for someone. More such jobs that are in fast-growing demand, but that might involve more direct oversight of you as an employee are:

Shipping/Receiving Clerk. Average wage: $14.00.

Uber/Lyft, etc. If you have your own car, consider driving for Uber, Lyft, or whatever current companies are promoting such type of jobs. This even includes food delivery companies where people order groceries or meals. These jobs often include tips. I had one roommate, an elderly man, who drove for Uber. He made a good living at it, enough to pay his rent to me, as well as meaning he could save his social security check and bank it in a savings account in its entirety. Just make sure you check out what your car insurance covers, and any other legal items that may need to be considered.

Accountant. Average Wage: $31.00 per hour.

Bartending. Average wage: $10.00 per hour, but remember all those tips, as well!

Restaurant Hosting/Wait staff, etc. Average wage: $10.00 an hour for host, but as with the wait staff, tips at many restaurants add to this.

Construction Management/Onsite/Offsite. Average wage: $40.00 per hour.

Retail Supervisor. Average wage (median): $18.00 approximately.

Graphic Designer. Average wage: $21.00 per hour.

Hospitality industry, Hotel/Resort Desk Clerks. Average wage: $10.00 per hour.

Driver, Delivery/Service. Average wage: $14.00

Forklift/Material Moving. Average wage: $25.60 per hour.

There are many more such types of jobs in a huge variety of fields, and the Internet is now one of the best places to find them or post the particular job type you would like to do. Things to keep in mind:

1. Pick not only the job you feel best qualified to do, but also one you can tolerate doing. Because this is a second job, and so should be considered temporary, try not to make it too demanding a one. Burnout will come sooner if you pick a stressful type of work, or one that is physically demanding. Trust me; burnout always comes with second jobs. Working 50, 60, 70 hours a week will do that to a person after a while, like it or not.

2. Try to pick a job where you are not constantly overlooked and supervised too closely. Some actually prefer close supervision, but most find it uncomfortable, annoying, and often find it leads to personality clashes when the supervisor is constantly looking over one's shoulder. As a second job, you need to have a little more freedom and so less stress than you might have for your primary work.

In the final analysis, always, always remember that a second job will not be a permanent one. This is true in the vast majority of cases. No matter how easy a job may be, the sheer number of added hours will take their toll on you sooner or later. So when thinking about a second job, keep these points in mind:

A. Make sure you want a second job, if it is really worth it to you to go this route. If you have family, this can cause a lot of stress on them, as well as on you. You don't need to have a marriage end in divorce, for example! If your goal is to make your life better for you and your family, think carefully, because it might just end up by doing the opposite.

B. When you take a second job, have VERY set goals in mind as to what you intend to do with the money. When I had my second job, I had to have a "light at the end of the tunnel," a day when I knew I would no longer need it, in order to keep working the long hours two jobs created for me in the meantime. I set an end date, six months later, when I would give up my second job. Of course, when the time came, I found that very difficult to follow through on, because I still felt I needed the money. That is the trap of a second job—it's hard to let go of it when the time comes!

C. Don't get sidetracked with the extra money. There is a

GREAT natural tendency to let the income produced by a second job filter into the everyday expenses of you and your family's lives. DO NOT DO THIS! Keep the money separate in all ways. Whatever debts you earmarked it for, or whatever investment you want the funds to go to, keep on track with those things! Otherwise, your extra money will just evaporate and you won't know where it's gone. Furthermore, you will be no closer to getting out of your indebtedness than you were before you took the second job. If the money is to be used as investment, it must go to that investment! If you do not do this, stick to your goals with regard to this added income, you defeat the whole purpose of having a second job.

Now, having said this, let's move on to the second part of increasing your income.

CHAPTER SEVEN

*The Sixth Step — Part Two
— Creating A Business*

After having seen the plus and minuses of getting a second job to increase your income, it's time to consider another method of going about creating more money for yourself and ultimately, this is the better one. What is it? Well, simply put, this is by starting your own business. As mentioned in the prior chapter, getting a second job may be the first step in achieving this goal, of acquiring the funds to start such a business. However, a second job should never be your final goal, or be considered as a permanent solution.

Now don't panic. Many of us think of starting a business as a daunting task, a major operation, and one that will suck up all your time and effort. Moreover, most of us fear the amount of risk involved in doing such a thing.

However, try to think of a "business" in the larger sense of the term. A simple example is if your son or daughter does a little mowing of some neighbors' lawns. That's a business. Of course, such a business is neither complicated, expensive, nor daunting.

MOST OF US DREAM OF HAVING OUR OWN BUSINESSES OF WORKING FOR OURSELVES! And why not? What could be better than being your own boss, making your own money, and being a success at what you have chosen to do? These are great incentives for starting your own business and they are not the only ones. Moreover, again, the definition of what you think of as a business should be expanded. For some, a business might be just taking any extra cash they have and investing it carefully in the stock market. For others, it might involve becoming a real estate agent and eventually having your own real estate company, locally, regionally, or whatever. So a business is hardly always about producing some material product, boxing it up, distributing and selling it. Although, that can be an ideal way to go for many.

CAVEAT: Starting businesses will cost in time and effort, and some can be financially draining. Moreover, you will still have to answer to others, even if it's only the demands of your own family. So do keep this in mind when contemplating starting a business. Businesses need commitment, time, and often money to get them going. However, the returns can be marvelous!

So, how does one start a business. Well, we are back to those basic steps again. Here they are:

1. Take stock of your talents, abilities, and assets. As always, this is the first step in any endeavor when it comes to increasing your income. Furthermore, you might be surprised at just what you are capable of as an individual, and what might actually turn out to be assets for a business in the material form. For instance, do you collect baseball cards? I know a man who collected so many, he opened his own store and online business in baseball cards and made a success of it. The same sort of thing would apply to lots of other types of collections, vinyl records, dolls, automobile accessories—you name it, there is usually a market for it all! So check out what it is you have in the way of material advantages to help you start a business, and also what your talents are. There are lots of places online already set up to sell you goods, such as EBay and Etsy.

CAVEAT: When taking stock, it's not enough just to say: "Oh, I have a lot hood ornaments for old cars my last husband left here. I could sell those." If you don't like selling hood ornaments, don't have an interest in them, then this probably isn't the way for you to go on a permanent basis. However, by selling those ornaments, you could get the money you need to start the business you do want to try your hand at.

Nevertheless, **ALWAYS REMEMBER, YOU SHOULD LIKE WHATEVER IT IS YOU DO!** If you do not like doing something, your interest will quickly wane and worse, you will be stuck in something you don't like and perhaps for quite some while. If that's the case, you might as well keep a job you don't like! Often, it's easy to get involved in a moneymaking arrangement, but not so easy to then get out of it. Extricating yourself from a business can be time consuming and sometimes complicated. That's why you must consider carefully just what type of business you want to do. Otherwise, you could end up by being very unhappy with your life!

Yet, a business can be profitable and quite quickly if you pick the right one. An example:

When I moved from a sleepy little retirement town to St. Petersburg, Florida, I sold my home. This gave me $65,000 in cash equity. As nice a sum as this seemed at the time, the price of homes in St. Petersburg, on average for a decent one, started at more than this and of course, only went up from there. Prices are usually higher in a city.

Furthermore, this money represented my life's savings. If I invested it wrongly, that was it. There was no more. If I chose a home in the wrong area, I could lose much of my equity (as many did during the Great Recession). Therefore, I had strongly to consider how I should invest what money I had left.

I made a decision. I decided the safest way to approach the whole issue was to look for a property that not only had a home for me on it, but at least some sort of rental(s), as well, to help defray the cost of owning the home, and perhaps even make me a little money besides.

I decided on buying a five-plex, a remodeled, large, and older home in "the Old Northeast" section of St. Petersburg. The regulatory laws at the time, regarding what constituted a full rental business (with regard to taxes and city regulations) versus owning just a couple of rentals had a limit of four rental units before things got "complicated."

However, since I occupied by far the largest unit myself, I was an onsite owner, thus able to get a standard residential bank loan, since there were only four units for rent, not a commercial-rated one of five units or more, which would have meant higher rates and again, different city regulations regarding the property.

There was a problem. The property was just over $100,000 and this was after some extensive negotiation on my part. Moreover, it was older and a bit rundown. Still, the property became mine, since I had the $65,000 and so used the biggest portion of that as a down payment. The first thing I did was try to "spruce up the property." I had kept some cash, not having used all of it in the purchase of the property. I put up a privacy fence around the property. I added a large Jacuzzi. I installed electric doorbell buzzers on the outer gate at the front of the property that chimed at each apartment unit.

If people wanted to visit someone on the premises, they had to buzz the number of the apartment in question and then wait for the person to come down and open the gate for them. The gate was self-locking when shut. I also, and this might raise some eyebrows, made the interior area of the grounds clothing optional. Although few tenants availed themselves of this extra feature, prospective tenants loved the idea. You see, I rented to young adults, mostly separated or divorced, and the small one-bedroom units I had, I described as "apartments for singles or the divorced" in my advertisements. I also kept the rents at a moderate rate. The truth was, I needed to fill those rental units and fast. I needed the money!

The apartments took off! In the matter of a month or so, I had all the rental units filled. Now I had the income to do upgrades for the tenants, like carpeting the hallways and apartments with new carpet, painting, repairs, etc. Even so, I had extra cash. The extra money not only paid my mortgage and all the utilities, but also left me extra besides!

As the apartments' qualities improved, and there was turnover (as there always is with rentals), I could then raise the rents accordingly, although I always tried to keep this to a moderate level. Before long, I had a waiting list of people wanting to rent an apartment. This was important news. It meant my rents were too low. So I raised the rental rates some more, but never too much. I wanted full apartments as much as possible. High rents could mean a long time between prospective renters.

Moreover, I didn't have to pay hardly a thing to advertise! I simply put up business cards, specially designed to push the good points of my apartments on bulletin boards in various nightclubs and bars where singles, divorced and separated people tended to go. I passed out business cards along with tips at restaurants, etc. Before long, this strategy worked so well, I bought a second five-unit building. Within two years, I was then able to buy a triplex, as well. Then I bought a duplex! The rental incomes from the existing properties helped me with qualifying to purchase yet more such properties. It was a snowball effect.

Two important things here; I went for a niche rental market and it worked. Furthermore, I did not purchase properties all in the same area of the city, but dispersed them around the entire metropolis. If one area went down in value for some reason, this way, another area going up in value might compensate. I was not one to put all my eggs in one local neighborhood basket.

I also had to hire help. I hired a part-time handyman as an independent contractor, although I did much of the simple stuff myself (painting, mowing, bookkeeping, etc.), and hired professional electricians and/or plumbers when needed. St Petersburg allowed homeowners to do their own work without problems (meaning city permits), but required permits if contractors did the work. This only applied to the exterior of buildings, though, and the interiors were not subject to such rules. In any case, I was big on avoiding such hassles and the attendant inspectors as much as possible and to do so legally. Dealing with bureaucracy unnecessarily was never something I liked to do.

Finally, after some eight years of doing this, and making a good deal of money in the process, I decided to call it quits. I no longer wanted to be a landlord and instead, now having the sufficient funds to do so, decided I wanted to turn my hand to writing. I sold all the properties and left Florida to do this, wanting a somewhat cooler environment to live and write in. I ultimately ended up buying two acres with a home on it within a very short distance of a very large lake (just one-tenth of a mile). This gave me the peace and quiet, the pleasant rural setting I wanted. I've been writing ever since.

I had taken what money I had, created a flourishing rental business out of it, and then sold it off so that I could proceed to what I ultimately, really wanted to do, and that was writing. So my writing isn't what made me my money to begin with, but rather rental properties. However, writing continues to make me money now.

Therefore, starting a business can be fairly easy, and making money off of it can come very quickly, indeed! My personal advice is never buy a single-family home until you are of a certain advanced age, perhaps retirement age. Buy at least a duplex or two units of some type. The income from one will pay all of the mortgage, taxes and insurance for both units in many cases, if you buy right. So you get to live in the other unit entirely for free. This means a lot of freed-up income for you! It also means you are gaining equity in the property at no cost to you personally.

If you go with a triplex, you can even make a good profit! Even if this is just three, side-by-side condos, it's a good idea. That way, you can be on site, always act as your own manager, and keep an eye on your properly. Truly, homes can make you money, but if you buy a single-family home and you and your family are the only ones living in it, then that house is just a cost to you, a financial burden. Even as an asset, it is long range, because it takes time to build equity. Make your properties work for you in some way!

CAVEAT: I quickly learned, as many landlords do, that you have to be actively involved in managing your properties. I had tried several management agencies at different times, and the truth is, I found none of them did the job as well as I, myself, did. The old adage about "never being an absentee landlord" was true in my case.

You should be active in any rental property business you do, not just passive. And a bit of personal advice here; with the retail apocalypse going on, the closing of more stores year after year, I would stay away from buying such properties. There is a reason they are so cheap to buy, and empty when you are looking at them!

Therefore, although the idea of starting a business can be scary because of such pitfalls, just first think carefully how you want to go about it. I just rather fell into it, and even that worked well for me and despite a few pitfalls along the way!

2. Pick a business you would love or at least like to do. Find something you love doing and try to make a business around that. This way, what to others might be work and drudgery, is for you a magnificent obsession! One of the main reasons to start a business, besides the obvious one of making money, is to be able to do what you really like doing and also being your own boss. So think carefully about what it is you would like to try your hand at before committing to it.

Give yourself time to contemplate this subject, to think it through; because once you commit to something, you should truly be committed to making a go of it! You can't enter a plan with only lukewarm enthusiasm. That's a sure recipe for failure if you do!

3. Once you've picked what it is you would like to try to make money at, you then need to pick a venue. In other words, how are you going to go about selling whatever it is that you plan on selling, whether services or material products? The truth of the matter is, and I don't think I'm overstressing this, because one of the best ways of selling these days is through the Internet. Unless you absolutely have to have a brick and mortar store to sell what it is you want to, you save an incredible amount of money by not having to lease/rent a building or shop, pay utilities, property taxes, and/or pay a regular support staff to man the place.

As mentioned, many standard brick and mortar stores are in big trouble these days, and this includes many of the biggest chains. The Gap, The Banana Republic, Sears, J.C. Pennys, and so many more. They are all struggling to keep their heads above water. In fact, it is predicted that sometime this year, Sears may cease to exist as a company altogether if things don't improve quickly for them.

Moreover, many stores have collapsed. Anyone care to remember the fate of Blockbuster Videos? Tower Records? Circuit City? They all suffered dire fates when online businesses and/or the digital revolution came into its own.

The Internet spelled their demise, just as surely as it has done so for many other businesses. This is an ongoing process, continuing to happen, as well. Many brick and mortar stores, unless selling something truly unique that simply can't be purchased over the Internet, are going this sad way.

What was the problem? Declining numbers of people visiting the stores/malls, and yet the businesses still had to pay high, square-footage overhead, utilities, taxes, and employees' wages and benefits. In short, they just couldn't compete with the online businesses that could afford to sell their products more cheaply because they didn't have this high an overhead.

My advice, if you can do your business via the Internet, then do so! It is one of the cheapest ways going, as far as costs are concerned. Whether a service, a physical product, or whatever, try to see if you can do it via the Internet before going any other route.

Don't forget, there are many websites already set up, such as EBay and others, where you can sell just about anything, and for a small fee. This beats the heck out of paying to rent a store, praying you get enough foot traffic, and that your monthly utility and employee fees aren't so high as to steal all of your profit! The same holds true for services you might wish to supply. Here is a list of some such sites in no particular order:

Upwork (writers/programmers/editors/copywriters, etc.)
Craigslist (more than just for buying and selling
Freelanced
FlexJobs
Damango
Demand Studios
Smashing Jobs

Fourerr
Findeavor
Freelancer
Workhoppers
RedGage
Genuine Jobs
Scribendi
Findeavor
Gigblasters
Gigbucks
Guru
Help Cove
iFreelance
IMGiGz
Freelance Writing Jobs
Gigdollars
Fiverr
Just Answer
JobBoy
Mechanical Turk
Workhoppers
Microworkers
Gigbux
Greatlance
Behance
Tutor
Minijobz
People Per Hour
TenBux
RapidWorkers
Task Army
Short Task
Student Freelancing
Taskr
Staff
We Work Remotely

Art Wanted
Writer Bay
DesignCrowd
Freelance Writing Gigs
Authentic Jobs
Envato Studio
Government Bids
Journalism Jobs
YunoJuno
Online Writing Jobs
Problogger Jobs
TextBroker
Triond
Toptalamango
Zeerk
99Designs
TopCoder
CrowdSpring
Programmer Meet Designer
Coroflot
Project4Hire
Smashing Jobs
Field Nation
Computer Assistant
Geniuzz
Get A Coder
Hexi Design
Joomlancers
SEO Clerks

As with many sites on the web, these are correct as of the writing of this book. Names change for some of them, as an example, Upwork used to be known as Elance. And such sites can come and go over time. Neither am I recommending any site in particular over another, or saying one might be better than another might be. It just depends on what type of service you want to provide as to which job sites might be best for you.

Also, the type of work available at these sites varies, but overall, this is a highly diverse list, including everything from writing, art, programmers, designers, coders, audio, video, various projects, SEO, tutoring—well you name it—one or more of these sites probably has it. Moreover, the above is only a partial list. There are many more such sites!

4. Create a business plan. For many, the idea of creating a business plan is a showstopper right off the bat. The idea, the intricacies involved, the research and the rest scare many people away from wanting to start a business. This is understandable. It's not an easy task, and for many, it is truly daunting.

However, there are two ways to go about this. The first is to create a standard business plan (and there is plenty of free help online to do this) if you want to try to get a loan or loans to start your new business. This is necessary. Banks, for instance, won't touch you without a detailed business plan to refer to.

Still, many of us aren't looking to go further into debt by obtaining loans to start our own businesses. Even so, a basic business plan is a marvelous tool to help you succeed in your endeavors. So the second way is just to come up with a business plan that will help you, personally, to know how to go about what you intend to do. Plans can tell you much, as in who the target buyers of your goods or services will be, so how to advertise, what your expected profit will be, as well as your costs, etc.

Additionally, it helps you to know when you will need to expand, when you might need to hire help—well, all sorts of things one should know when starting a business. Furthermore, all this is important stuff to know when creating your own business and it more often than not makes the difference between being a success in your enterprise, versus being a failure.

Currently, it is estimated that (according to the Small Business Administration) that half of newly started businesses manage to survive for at least five years, and around a third can make it well past the ten-year mark. These are remarkably good statistics, because it used to be thought most businesses (95 percent of them), failed in the first three to five years. That's the good news. The bad news is that new businesses still fail all too often.

How do you avoid being part of such a dismal statistic? Well, for one thing, by making sure you do your groundwork, picking something you love to do, and committing to it, and having a good business plan. Also, if there is someone you are sure is reliable to help you in the business, to be a partner with you in your endeavor, that's a big help, as well. Partnerships can be very useful, but there are also some major problems with them to consider. I'll discuss this in the next Chapter.

CHAPTER EIGHT

Part 3 — Partnerships

The Power of Partnerships. Partnerships, if done right, can be incredibly helpful in starting your own business and also help to defray costs. When they work right, partnerships speed up the process enormously and allow you to expand your business much faster than you might otherwise. I had a partner in my real estate business and it did wonders for accelerating the growth of my rental business and increasing the income from it accordingly.

Example: If someone wants to flip houses (yes, people are now doing that again) to make money, the first thing one has to do is to be able to afford the home they want to then flip. That takes money, and money takes time to accumulate as we all know too well. However, with a partner, this process speeds up. For instance, if two people who have the same income can manage to save the same approximate amounts over a similar timespan, then buying that first house would only take half the time. If it would take you two years to gather the funds for that first down payment, it would only take a year if two people were working and saving equal amounts of money to do this. Thus, you'd have the house in one year, instead of two, and could then proceed to flip it much more quickly.

Additionally, that's just the time factor for coming up with the money to start a business. The time factor also works to you and your partner's advantage if you both put in the same effort and time in repairing/upgrading the home. Two can get work done much more swiftly and more easily than one. It always helps if someone is holding the ladder for you, so to speak.

Therefore, partnerships can be a great boon to speeding up the whole process of getting your business going and then quickly being able to expand it. As the old saying goes, "two heads are better than one," and "many hands make for light work." This is a truism.

Partnerships are very good in this way, for they help with the work, the time factor, and the pitfalls. One person might just see a business danger where another might not. In my case, this was true. I needed a practical-minded person, one I could trust implicitly and I was lucky enough to have one. My rental business couldn't have moved so quickly, been so successful in so short a time, if this had not been the case. For me, a partner was an absolute necessity.

CAVEAT: As wonderful as a good partnership can be, **THERE CAN BE MAJOR PROBLEMS WITH THE WRONG PARTNERSHIP.** Do you need proof of this? Well, here is a very sobering statistic:

Up to 80% Of Business Partnerships Fail!

That's a staggeringly high number, and it means that you only have one chance in five to succeed in a business partnership, or to reverse this, there are four out of five chances the partnership will fail. That's high by anyone's standards!

However, this statistic doesn't tell the whole story. First, this is an overall number that includes every type of business partnership. The statistic isn't broken down into partnerships based on types, such as those based on long friendships, spouses, or relatives, versus business partnerships with strangers and/or investors. In other words, the type of relationship between the partners can have a strong influence on whether the partnership works out well or not.

This also means that the failure rate could be much higher between people who are just acquaintances, business or otherwise, who start a partnership, whereas, the failure rate can be much lower when the partnerships are based on spouses, family, and/or good, long-term friends.

This is not to say that friends don't fall out in business partnerships! They do and more often than any of us would like to admit. Moreover, one often loses the friend in the process. This can and does happen at times with spouses and significant others, as well. However, overall, the stronger the bond between the persons involved, the more long-term it has been, the better the chances of the business partnership succeeding.

Examples:

A Bad Partnership. Two friends I knew in San Diego, California, decided to form a partnership to create what they felt would be a thriving business—plants for landscaping on the commercial and private level, a plant nursery. They wanted to buy some land with an agricultural zoning outside the city limits (and therefore, the city's taxation system) of San Diego, but still close enough to allow for a good business trade to develop. There, they would use the land initially to grow exotic plants then in high demand in Southern California. These plants would include various types of palm trees, cycads, and flowering trees, such as the African Tulip Tree, Jacaranda, and others.

Once the business started making a profit, they planned to open a garden center on the property, as well. Here, they could sell other items besides just the plants, including plant pots, fertilizers, etc., and so diversify their profit base.

On the face of it, this was an excellent idea. One of them, who worked for City Parks and Recreation, certainly had the expertise in the form of a long career as a gardener for the city, and later working his way up to be the City Horticulturist.

The other, an art teacher, felt that his ability to cast pottery would make a good secondary source of income for the business plan, since those who bought "potted palms" would probably want the right size decorative pots for them, as well. He taught ceramics at his school, and somehow (I'm not sure how), was able to keep most of the product the high school kids came up with.

Based on this premise, the two purchased two acres north of San Diego. They set about creating a supply of stock plants to move to the land to grow to the larger versions needed for landscaping contractors, as well as smaller versions for sale to the public in general. The horticulturist rented the backyards of several neighbors in his area and potted up palms by literally the thousands.

The schoolteacher helped with the seedlings to some degree. However, as it turned out, things began to go wrong. The schoolteacher, not enthused with the plant end of the business, left a great deal of the actual physical labor of potting up the thousands of seedlings and then maintaining them (watering, fertilizing, etc.) to the horticulturist, saying that he could get his class to start making more pots that way, which they could then later sell, as well. Yet, the numbers of pots produced were only in the dozens, and the size of them was, more often than not, too small to hold anything but tiny palm trees, but no other plants of any real size.

Things came to a head when they decided to have a major yard sale to generate needed cash. They wanted to install a water sprinkling system, among other things, on the acreage, or at least, the horticulturist thought this was the reason for the sale, since he had proposed the idea and for that reason. The partner had agreed to this at the time. The yard sale was also to see how they could work together on the retail end, a test, as it were.

Unfortunately, it didn't work very well. While the horticulturist and a friend of his sold plenty of palm trees and did all the work, the teacher, along with his friend/aide, were barely around at all. In fact, the man, known to be a drinker, had brought over a gallon jug of wine and was often inside the horticulturist's house drinking tumblers of the stuff, rather than helping with the sales outside. His aide simply drove off, not wanting anything to do with the whole project, as it turned out.

Therefore, while two people worked diligently to make the sale a success, and ultimately did, the other partner did little and had brought little product to sell. Yet, at the end of the day, he demanded 50% of the proceeds, even though his share of the sales came to only about 15% and he had done very little work. Rather than argue over this, the horticulturist agreed to split the income evenly, although irritated, because he had thought the money was to be used for the property, and not the private use of the schoolteacher or himself. Moreover, most of the proceeds had come from his efforts, and not the teacher's.

This was a revelation for the horticulturist. The schoolteacher, who had seemed originally enthused and promised to make up for his lack of expertise in the exotic landscape business by paying in labor, had not kept his part of the bargain at all, at least not as far as the horticulturist was concerned. Moreover, the miserably few number of pots that sold also showed the horticulturist that such a contribution in product by the teacher would be of little real value in such a business. Palm trees of any size simply would need bigger containers, ones the art teacher's kilns could not accommodate.

Furthermore, the horticulturist, although knowing his friend drank, hadn't realized just how extensive his drinking had become over the years until the day of the sale. The man had hidden this well, apparently. Therefore, the horticulturist, after confronting and discussing all this with the teacher, decided to end the partnership. This meant the land, still unused for its original purposes, could be sold, or so the horticulturist thought....

The teacher balked at this idea of selling the property. He felt the land (his 50 percent share of it), was a good investment, and if left alone over the coming years (for land was skyrocketing in price in the San Diego area at the time), would make for a valuable inheritance for his children.

The horticulturist countered that he could do nothing with the land, since the teacher owned an undivided half interest in the total property and so could be stopped and hindered at every turn if he tried to do something with the land.

Moreover, they had agreed to purchase the land for a business, and a specific one at that. Since the business was no longer possible, he argued the land should be sold, since its sole original purpose was no longer valid and he had no children he wanted to inherit the property, so why should he be stuck paying taxes on unusable land for years to come?

The two were at an impasse. They had land together, but a failed business partnership and no business. Selling the land seemed impossible without the consent of both parties to such a sale. In desperation, the horticulturist turned to attorneys to resolve the issue. This is what usually ultimately happens in such situations. At some point, attorneys always seem to end up entering the fray in such types of disputes.

Since the horticulturist had access to a powerful corporate law firm, he more or less won the day. The two signed a letter of agreement, he and the schoolteacher, to sell the land within one year of the date of the letter, if either party still wanted to at that point. They would seek the advice of three real estate agents to determine the value of the property at that time.

The year passed, and the sale finally proceeded. The land sold for well over what they had paid for it, but this was no surprise with property values skyrocketing as they had been. The two parted company. Not only was the business partnership at an end, but so was the friendship, as well, for all real purposes. Although still on hospitable terms with each other, there acquaintanceship never returned to what it had once been. Although, it had never been a deep one, their friendship had existed up until that point for the better part of two decades.

Therefore, not only the business partnership failed, but so did a long-term, and if not deep friendship, then at least a good acquaintanceship had gone, as well.

The only good to come of this was that the horticulturist, who had done by far and away most of the potting up of thousands of palm trees, and having even collected all the seed to do the potting, also became the sole owner of them. The teacher wanted no part of the labor involved in moving any of them to a new location, or maintaining them. In any case, he simply did not own them in any way.

The horticulturist grew them up for a couple of more years and later sold then in bulk, the entire quantity, to the San Diego Zoo and Wild Animal Park, which wanted them for their animal habitats there. Most of the planting material was "natural" and native to the environments the zoo had created for any number of the more tropical animal species they had. African tulip trees for African animals, as it were.

So although this partnership was dissolved in the end, and the hardworking partner made good from it all, ultimately, the upset, disagreements, and legal battles that had ensued for more than a year had taught him a valuable lesson—to be very careful about whom he formed business partnerships with!

An Example of a Good Business Partnership. Following along with this same horticulturist, he shortly later took an early retirement from the city and moved to Florida. There, the two of us met and later formed a real estate partnership, as mentioned earlier, and bought, refurbished, and then fully leased rental properties. Later, as mentioned earlier, we then sold them at a good profit. With this business partnership, the two of us were able to come up with the cash in one year to buy our first such property, rather than each of us, individually, having to wait several years to realize the necessary funds to do this.

This meant we could buy our properties much sooner and realize profits on investments that much sooner, as well, consequently. We both agreed the profits initially should be plowed back into the business, which we did. Within a matter of just three years, we had multiple properties. Our rental units expanded from none to 30 in that time, and were in different locations around the city. We had great tax write-offs and good income from them.

By the end of five years, the partnership was capable of buying a high-rise apartment building, if it so chose. We came close to doing this, but then each of us decided we'd had enough of being landlords. Therefore, as one of our real estate agents put it, we put the properties up for sale, sold them quickly, and "took the money and ran."

This business partnership had never had problems to speak of, other than the usual ones that one encounters with rentals—keeping them in a good state of repair, dealing with tenants who didn't pay on time, some evictions, etc. However, as for the two of us, we had no problems between us at all. In fact, we relied heavily on each other's strengths and expertise to expedite solutions to various problems. Some of these fell under the purview and knowledge of one of us more than the other, so this system worked very well for us.

Conclusion: So you can see that business partnerships, although they can have **MAJOR PITFALLS,** can work out, and work out well! The right business partners can make money. They can make it quickly, and in large amounts. In fact, good business partners can save years of time and great amounts of effort in succeeding in achieving their goals.

Where one owner might work himself literally to death trying to make a go of an enterprise, two or more partners can much more easily handle that workload and any attendant problems that could arise. Moreover, partners often contribute much in the way of fresh ideas, better ways to do things, and so help to increase the profits and make the business more efficient in many ways. Partners can be a great way to go! That is, if they can get along and work as a team.

So how does one find the right business partner? First, think carefully who might be a good partner for you. Just because they have been a long-term, close friend, doesn't mean they might make for a good business relationship. As with the horticulturist, he found his friend's enthusiasm for the idea quickly waned in the face of the physically demanding and tedious manual labor involved in the project. What's more, the horticulturist also found out his friend had much more of a drinking problem than he had realized. Ultimately, these things spelled the downfall of the partnership.

This often is the case. The stress of partnerships can cause all sorts of cracks in relationships, and sometimes even more importantly, under such strains, reveal more about your business partner than you ever suspected might have existed, and often would have preferred not to have existed! Sometimes, this can be a good surprise, true, but many times, it turns out to be a bad one. This latter happens more often than not, I'm afraid.

Therefore, above all else, place great importance on who you pick as a business partner, if you choose to have one. The choice will have great effect on whether your business rockets to a success, or founders on divisive issues and personalities involved in the partnership. So whom should you pick for a business partner? Well, again, only you can decide this, but here are some general guidelines:

Your business partner should be someone you have known for some while, if possible. Yes, a new person, one who is enthusiastic and has proven themselves to be a hardworking individual can work out well, too, but again, you are, as they say, "buying a bit of a pig in a poke," since you can't possibly know how this person will behave in a partnership relationship, or under stress. So:

1. Choose someone you feel you know well enough to risk (and there is risk involved, most definitely), in creating a business partnership.

2. Choose someone who not only has enthusiasm for the idea of the business, but also someone you are fairly sure is a hard worker, who will behave well under stress, and not throw in the towel at the first sign of trouble. You might even want to have a test or probationary period to establish this fact as true.

3. Choose someone you feel is honest. This might seem obvious, but this is a very important thing; it's not enough to "sort of" trust someone. You have to trust them implicitly and completely. Misplaced trust is a hard and painful lesson to learn. The actress, Doris Day, for example, trusted her business manager, who she'd known for a very long time, with handling all her finances.

So much did she value and trust him that she seldom checked

on what he was doing with her money. Well, he was doing something with it all right. He transferred the vast bulk of it to his name, embezzling almost all her wealth in the process, and then he fled to Brazil to live there comfortably and spend it all. Meantime, an aging actress, now virtually penniless, had to start again from scratch. She never did fully recover from that expensive bout of misplaced trust.

You will be trusting that your business partner will be honest with the money, inventory, and much else. You have to be sure you are able to trust them completely! So choose wisely and only after due consideration before you pick a partner. Otherwise, the results can be disastrous.

On the flipside, if you find a good partner, it makes for a wonderful boost, in not only your productive capability, but also how quickly your business can grow, expand, and become profitable. Two horses pulling a cart are better than one horse, especially on difficult roads. To push the metaphor further, two horses also make for a lighter load and faster traveling time. So give it some thought, a lot of thought, and then decide if a partnership is right for you.

CHAPTER NINE

Part 4 — Going It Alone

Because partnerships can be wonderful, we all gravitate to such an idea, but for many people, a partnership may not be the way to go. They simply may not want anyone else involved in the control of the business. There are still types of partnerships that allow for this and the main one is a general partnership.

As defined by Devin Scott, Michael Kupfer in their article on the subject at DelawareInc.com (See, References):

"A general partnership is the most common type of partnership. It refers to a relationship in which all partners contribute to the day-to-day management of the business. Each partner will have the authority to make business decisions and even legally bind the company in contracts.

The liabilities, contributions, and responsibilities of the partners are often equal unless stated otherwise. Typically, a partnership agreement will describe which partners have certain authorities and responsibilities."

This is the type of partnership I've been discussing up until now. There is also another type of partnership, a limited partnership, and this is also defined by Devin Scott and Michael Kupfer as:

"A limited partnership is a relationship where one or more part-ners are not involved in the day-to-day management of the business. Often, a limited partner, sometimes known as a "silent partner," will serve solely as an investor in the business, with the funds that they contribute being the extent of their liability. However, since the limited partner does not have decision-making power in the company, with-drawing funds – even just the amount they've already contributed – cannot be done without the approval of a general partner."

The article at the DelawareInc.com website goes into more specific detail on this subject and if you are interested in pur-suing this topic, I recommend you go to that site. However, the point here is that most partnerships people form are often of the general partnership variety, rather than the limited partnership. However, if you want total control of the business then a limited partnership isn't a bad way to go.

Yet, some people, many people in fact, would prefer to simply go it completely alone. This has its drawbacks in that it is just you doing all the work, fronting all the money for expenses, etc., but it does give you complete and absolutely control of your busi-ness. One way of approaching such a go-it-alone business is not to try for too much too soon, or to use the old proverb, "don't bite off more than you can chew." Still, even with smaller business, there is good money to be made if that's what you want to do.

As an example, I knew a woman that loved gardening, just the average, at-home, style gardening, but she also liked to grow small exotic plants. She determined she wanted to make money at it. However, how could she go about this? She was on a limited income, only had so much land to use (her house lot), and a limited means to distribute her products.

Furthermore, she had to find some type of plant or plants that people would be willing to buy that weren't already cheaply and easily available at nearby home improvement or box stores. Fi-nally, she also couldn't afford much in the way of distribution. So what was she to do?

The woman came up with an excellent answer. She would grow novelty plants, ones that would be popular for seasonal use, and also plants that wouldn't be too large, difficult, or too expensive to deliver. Her first such plant was an "egg tree." These could be grown in small pots, produced white, egg-shaped "eggs" the same size and look as a chicken egg, and which when finally turning yellow and ripe, could be eaten, and even resembled the taste of an egg.

Why was this seasonal? Because it was the perfect little Easter gift to give people because most had never heard of such a thing, eggs that grew on trees! What's more, she could grow them in six-inch pots, bare-root them, and mail them to people in standard plastic-coated, interior mailers at a minimal cost because of little weight and small size.

This turned out to be a money bonanza! She started small but eventually started selling so many, she filled her backyard with little pots of egg trees, all about six to twelve inches high. So popular did it become that when approached, even chain stores purchased them in bulk for Easter sales.

Needless to say, she made money! Lots of it! Furthermore, she didn't stop there. Instead, she also went for other exotic plants for various holidays, including St. Valentine's Day, Fourth of July, Halloween, Christmas (but not poinsettias—they were already a "drug on the market"), and even New Years! To say she had imagination and was inventive as to how she approached her business was an understatement.

However, she kept her business small, not wanting it to become too burdensome for her. Eventually, she even branched out into other types of plants, such as Venus Flytraps, Pitcher Plants, etc. One of her biggest and best selling ventures was a little longer term. When she discovered that Japanese Dwarf Maples sold in small containers for as much as $70.00 apiece, she planted a number of rows of those, as well. And yes, they sold very well!

She never expanded beyond her own backyard, though, and so easily kept control of her business, all aspects of it, and never required any other staff. She loved gardening so this was a labor of love for her, and it proved a very profitable one, indeed. Although, she did complain about the frequent trips to the post office....

So going it alone can work and work well, depending on how large a business you want, whether you want others involved or not, and whether it is more a way of making cash from a lucrative hobby, as it was with her. So the choice is yours! Partnership, or go it alone, making money works if you approach the task in the right way!

Egg Tree plant, Public Domain

So give the idea of just having you run the business, with nobody else, some real thought. The drawbacks are that it takes more work on your part, will probably take longer to get up and running, as well as longer in making a good profit. Still, you avoid the problem of having a partner that way. And as mentioned earlier, partnerships have a high rate of failure. Their rewards can be wonderful. They were for me. However, they can also create all sorts of personality conflicts, struggles for control, and even end in legal battles. Think carefully about which way you wish to proceed with your business for these reasons.

CHAPTER TEN

Part 4 — A Business Idea
To Make Money

No matter how carefully you plan, no matter how much research you do, taking that big step of actually starting a business, whether in selling a product or service, is a necessarily very big step. So it is important not to just jump into it without first doing a few important things. These are:

The Thinking Stage:

1. Consider very carefully if your idea for starting a business is a valid one in the sense that it is something you can stick with, be devoted to, and will want to do for quite a while to come. Don't just think, "Hey, I have a great idea" and then jump right into it. Ponder your idea. Think it over. Think it through. Discuss it with those you trust.

Try to extrapolate if there will really be a demand for whatever service or product you are thinking about providing. Consider the consequences of success and failure. Even test the idea on a small scale, if you can. Again, talk it over with friends, relatives or even a professional consultant. This last is important, to get some input from people you trust to be good advisors, whether friends, family, or again, some professional in which you place your trust.

However, also beware that others might give you false negative input, simply because they are afraid you might succeed! *Weltanschauung*, the German word for "delighting in another's misery," is a very real thing. People get jealous of those who strive to succeed, because from their point of view, it means they aren't doing their best to do so! Jealousy, plain and simple.

CAVEAT! Be careful with whom you discuss your business idea. If your idea is a good one, and the person turns out to be untrustworthy, they might very well steal it and beat you to it. This has happened more times in history than can be counted.

Whether a patent for an invention, a new product to market, or a new type or style of service, people have had their ideas stolen from them! Business is competitive. Even major corporations, such as major car companies have stolen ideas. Yes, they have been sued and sometimes they lose to the individual doing the suing, but trust me when I say this takes lots of money, a great deal of time, and much stress on your part to accomplish.

As Napoleon Hill said in his book, *Think And Grow Rich,* "before you tell the world what you are going to do, first show them!"

This is **VERY** important. There is a practical reason for it, so again, be very careful with whom you discuss your business idea. **PICK THE WRONG PERSON TO CONFIDE IN, AND YOU COULD LOSE OUT TO THAT PERSON, or at least, have a serious competitor you might never have had otherwise!** Competition will come soon enough anyway. If something works, people will rush to copy the idea. Ever notice that at some road junction with a freeway, or perhaps an entrance or exit, how just one fast food restaurant is quickly followed by more of similar ilk and all clustered within yards of each other?

If it works for one, then there will be copycats. In fact, this is so common, it is a principle of real estate. However, you want to keep whatever head start you've got, and try to make the brand your own before this inevitably happens. **If you become known for a certain brand, then it is that much harder for newcomers to successfully compete with you.**

2. Think seriously about what it is you want to do for people, whoever they might be (your target demographic—that is, the people you want to aim your service or product at). Give this one lots of thought! Do some research on it! For instance, you might make more money selling a $15.00 product to the professional class (doctors, lawyers, teachers, or whatever), than trying to sell a cheaper $5.00 product to the working class. Alternatively, the reverse might be true.

3. Keep your business idea as simple as you can. The more complex the idea or plan, the more likely it will encounter more difficulties, roadblocks, and obstacles. Once you have the idea, do some research, if only via your computer, to determine if there is a real demand for what you have in mind. For some things, there is always a demand, it seems, but for others not. Sometimes, just doing a better job at something is enough to make a lot of money. You know the old saying, "build a better mousetrap and people will beat a path to your door." It may be a cliché, but that's only because it's true and has withstood the test of time.

Again, do research. Try to find out if what you have in mind can be profitable. The truth about this is a blunt one; in order to succeed, you have to have a product/service people need or want, or one that you can make them think they need or want. It's that simple, and yes, it's that hard, too.

Discerning what people want or need isn't always as easy as one thinks. Even that better mousetrap, despite the old saying, if you do make one, isn't necessarily true. If that better mousetrap is too expensive, you might only get a trickle of customers or none at all. It may be better, but people will often go for what's cheaper, even if it isn't as good.

Therefore, there are factors in whatever the product or service is that you wish to market. It has to be:

a. Useful in the sense people either need or want it.

b. It has to be readily available, so you must have a distribution method that can handle demand.

c. The quality of the product or service must be as good as you can reasonably make it.

d. The price must not be more than your target customers are willing to pay. Again, a person of low income might want a better mousetrap, but simply not be able to afford your price! And the wealthy don't bother. They just rely on exterminators who may or may not bother buying your mousetrap. So who then would buy your better mousetrap? The answer is, sadly, hardly anybody.

Here's an example of this: Did you know that there are different versions of cream-based cures for vaginal yeast infections? A strange question, I know, but there is a seven-day formula, a three-day formula, and a one-day formula. Now the next question is, if someone is suffering from this illness, why wouldn't they buy the quickest-acting cure for it, rather than suffer for more days on end?

The answer, when put to a female television audience was simple. The seven-day and three-day formulas were cheaper! So it's amazing what people will do to save money, even suffer longer when they could cure it in one day!

4. Think carefully as to how much work and/or expertise is involved in your business idea. Do you need a partner with greater expertise than you have in that regard? If so, again, think carefully as to whom you should turn to and make sure they, too, already are or can become as enthusiastic about the business as you are.

CAVEAT: Be very careful here. Many an entrepreneur, for lack of money or expertise, has turned to others for help, only to have them take the idea as their own and run with it. Often, these people have the finances or ready access to such and so can move more swiftly than you can. If your idea is a workable product that can be patented, you should do this as soon as possible. If your idea is more of a local business or service (specialty restaurant, etc.), make sure the person you talk to about it, as to being a possible partner, isn't the type to go ahead and proceed without you, or arrange the contract/partnership so that they can eventually assume control without your permission! This happens more often than one might realize.

Remember what I mentioned about competition? Remember the example that when a profitable fast food restaurant or business opens at a new location that it is a standard rule/proviso in real estate that competition will spring up around the new business, and in many cases, in less than a year or two? Many real estate brokers even inform their customers of this fact, as a warning.

When someone sees someone making a good profit, they are quick to follow the example. However, there are some unscrupulous people who will just advance your idea/plan to those with more money and who can act faster upon it than you can. While you search for someplace cheap to build your business, that same real estate agent can be selling that idea and location to a richer investor, thus upping his/her commission. Again, most real estate agents are honest, but like any profession, there are always those few who are not. Some will even back stab another agent involved to make a better commission.

When I was a real estate broker, a client approached me wanting to buy an empty business for a new enterprise. I found him one. The other agent involved in the deal, the one for the seller also worked for my firm. He immediately pushed to have me taken out of the deal, since he was supposedly the "commercial real estate agent" for our firm, and the only one. So he felt he should get the entire commission for this reason, although I was the one who had the buyer! His ploy didn't work, but it does show how people can get greedy and shove aside their ethics and morals when it comes to making money! So be careful. Needless to say, I would NEVER have trusted him as a business partner!

5. Once you have your idea and are ready to implement it, you are on your way! Now, in the next chapter it's time to implement your idea.

CHAPTER ELEVEN

Part 5 — The "Doing" Stage

All right, so by this point you have thought your idea over carefully. You have researched whether there is or can be a demand created for your service or product. You have also contemplated the idea of whether or not you initially need a partner. Moreover, you have bounced your idea off of people who are knowledgeable, but also ones you know you can trust.

Now, you are ready to start "doing." That is, you are actually ready to implement your business plan and idea. This, too, comes in stages.

First, do you require money to start your business idea? If so, you need to determine exactly how much money you need. If it isn't a large amount and/or you have the necessary funds, you can then proceed to the next stage, actually getting underway.

However, if you do not have the necessary funds, then you must seek out those who are willing to support you in your business, whether family, friends, or business partners. Either that, or get a second job to earn the money needed to start the business, or find it in some other way.

CAVEAT: Family and friends may loan you the necessary funds without demanding something in return. Business partners (and this includes banks), will want something in return, usually in

the form of interest of some sort, and this might also involve an eventual balloon payment after a certain period of time.

Be wary of that!

Others may just be willing to help but at too high a price! As with the television show, *Shark Tank*, and as they sometimes do, they might just demand too big a piece of the action for you to feel comfortable to agreeing to such terms. Only you can decide if what the business partner, bank, or whatever, in demanding the terms with regard to your business, are demanding terms you can live with, perhaps for years to come.

Sometimes, even when a business makes good money, most of the profits are siphoned off to those who have invested in the business. This means it can take a long time before you earn a decent income or profit off your idea, enough of a one to even sustain yourself while doing the business. The less money you need to make a go of it, the more "friendly" the source of any such investment funds in your business (such as relatives, etc.), and the better the terms and conditions of any possible loan, the better off you will be, of course!

Don't be discouraged! Most ideas to make money often require a good deal of effort on one's part, as well as some funding to get underway. However, if you have done the recommended assessment of taking stock of your finances, followed the course above I outlined to make yourself more solvent, you will be in a good position to get started on your plan, putting it into action. If you have a great idea, but it requires more funding than you can manage, you still have alternatives.

The first way is simply to put the idea away for a while and choose a less expensive one to start with. Once you make enough profit from this "smaller" idea, you can then trot out your original one and fund it at that point.

The second way is seeking funding from sources that won't demand too high a return on their investment in your idea. Crowd sourcing/funding is a great way to go about this method. You simply go online, present your idea in a well thought out manner to the general public at a website intended for the purpose, offer something (that you can live with) in return for the funds received, and sometimes this is very little, and hope your idea catches the imagination of citizens who might wish to contribute to your funding program. Some crowd sourcing/funding sites examples are:

Kickstarter
Indiegogo
Gofundme
Giveforward
Crowdwise
Kiva
Crowdrise
Patreon
Teespring

And many others exist besides these. Different sites specialize in funding different types of things. For instance, Teespring is primarily for getting funds for developing innovative T-shirts. I have a fellow author who successfully managed to get crowdfunding to have his book turned into a movie. I have another who had his trilogy of books crowdfunded to get them published. The price for these funds? The contributors received constant word on the state of the books' progressions, an invitation to attend a free kickoff party for contributors only, and a signed and numbered copy of each book in the trilogy. So there are many ways one can go about enticing contributors to support your business idea.

So the first thing you have to do in the doing stage is to actually come up with whatever funds you need to start your business. My advice is to always overestimate. Things come up, as "they" say, that one doesn't think will happen, so it's better to have a small surplus of funds to handle such unexpected contingencies, then face a problem for lack of such funds and so fall at the first hurdle or obstacle.

CHAPTER TWELVE

Part 7 — Putting Your Idea To Work

Once you have the funds and your idea to make money ready to go, it's time to actually get started with the process portion of your plan. You must purchase whatever it is you will need for your idea. We've been talking about products for sale as the standard business model here for making money, but another great way to make money is by providing a service. The advantages of offering a service is they can often be started with very little in the way of money.

A Case In Point: I had a friend who lost his job due to the Great Recession. He was out of work, had very little in the way of savings (only a few hundred dollars), and his bills were mounting, as were the demands for payment of those bills. With a family to support, he was initially at a loss as to what to do. Finding other work just wasn't working for him, because nobody was hiring. To say he was between the proverbial "rock and a hard place" was to understate things.

In desperation, he came up with an idea. He could start a cleaning service. This would have little initial cost to him, since all he required were some buckets, mops, brooms, a decent vacuum, cleaning supplies, and a few other minor accessories. My friend had no illusions about making a fortune off this, but just hoped he could make enough money to keep his head above water "for a while until the job market got better," as he put it.

He acquired the things he needed and placed advertisements on any free sites on the Internet, as well as on bulletin boards free at various supermarkets, etc. He hoped by doing this, he could attract homeowners who needed a cleaner, perhaps on a weekly or monthly basis. If he found enough of these sorts of jobs, he might just manage to meet his debt obligations and not lose his home. For this reason, he kept his prices low.

Then he seized upon another idea. He had business cards made up (some of these were posted on those same grocery store bulletin boards) and then went around to various small, medium, and large businesses, leaving them flyers and/or a business card. At first, nothing much happened for almost a month, and my friend grew despondent. He came close to giving up on the idea. However, since he had no other real options as he saw it, he continued his canvassing for work.

At last, he received some good news. In one week, after having again visited some of the same businesses to "remind them," as he put it, that he "existed," two small businesses gave him a call. One had lost their cleaner, and another had fired theirs. My friend took the two jobs, which were nightly. He emptied wastepaper baskets, vacuumed carpets, polished floors, cleaned bathrooms, and dusted. He didn't mind the work, because unlike his other job, these weren't demanding jobs in the mental sense, and there was little or no stress involved. Nor did he find the work physically demanding, either. For him, it was not much worse than cleaning one's own home.

The first few months went this way, with my friend making just enough money to meet some of his more pressing financial obligations. Then, business started picking up. Word of mouth was spreading about his reasonable rates and good work. Owners of businesses referred him to others. Soon, his wife, who had recently lost her job, as well, became part of his cleaning business. Together, they handled the increased workload well enough.

Then, his big break came. A corporate attorney office, an entire floor of a downtown high-rise, contacted him and asked if he would like to contract with them for cleaning their offices. Again, the work was not difficult, but it would take at least seven hours every night, but he decided to go for it. The money was good! VERY GOOD! Now, my friend and his wife were earning the equivalent of their former combined salaries and then some. They were becoming well off once more!

He contacted (through a referral from the corporate law firm) another business in the same building and ended up with two more floors to clean. Now my friend asked his teenage son and daughter if they could help out, but for pay, of course. They jumped at the chance to make some money and both worked part-time for their father and mother. This helped cover their college costs.

My friend's business kept growing. More major firms wanted him as a cleaning agency. He was now well established. However, he had reached the point where he had to bring in extra help. This was a problem. It wasn't due to a lack of available labor, but now he had to deal with actual hired help, and all the attendant administrative and accounting duties involved. My friend was not one for trying to figure out the legalities, such as how to withhold social security, workmen's compensation, or making payrolls, and such. However, his wife was willing to do this part of it. She gave up her part in the actual cleaning and became the business manager.

Over the next few years, the business grew until it became, if not "the cleaning agency" in the region, it was at least one of the top five. All this took a total of about three-and-one-half years to achieve. My friend created a million-dollar-plus, thriving business, one that he eventually sold for a tidy profit. He retired early, as did his wife and they now live very comfortably in the upscale neighborhood of Scottsdale, Arizona.

His principle interest these days, outside of his family, of course, is golfing, and Arizona/Scottsdale is world-renowned for its golf courses. The marvelous thing is that he can now afford to golf every day, travel as he pleases and anywhere he pleases, and live a lifestyle he never thought he would be able to afford. He did all this in just under four years! Truly, a rags to riches story.

Therefore, making money doesn't necessarily require some incredible idea for a new product or new type of business. My friend simply chose one he could afford, and one that was hardly new. This may sound like a Horatio Alger story of old, but it is a true one, nevertheless.

The point here is there were any number of ideas he might have come up with to make money. There always are. It's not as if there is just one magical idea that works. There are many! He picked one he could afford on the cheap, that took a minimum amount of cash to get started, and within his very meager budget, one that was simple, but one that worked! He didn't have to invent anything new. He didn't have to go on some show like **Shark Tank** and publicly beg for money, only to have them deny him, or only to have them take a lion's share of his business. He simply bought the tools he needed most, started very small, and quickly grew the business to a multimillion-dollar enterprise!

This is what you have to do. Find something that suits you, is within your budget, and is a workable idea. Some ideas are great, but they simply are too unwieldly to work without a great deal of funding. If you can find the funding—go for it! If you can't find the money, come up with an idea you financially can live with and afford as my friend did.

CAVEAT: Beware of The Ever-Lurking Peter's Principle:

"The Peter principle is an observation that in an organizational hierarchy, every employee will rise or get promoted to his or her level of incompetence."

—Ivestopedia

This is important, because although an old saying, a true cliché, it also happens to be very true. My friend found this is exactly what happened to him. As his business grew, his wife took on all the administrative tasks as mentioned, which she happened to be very good at. However, there was still the problem of him having to find employees he could trust. After all, when one works in corporate firms at night and alone, you have to have people you can trust not to steal or do damage.

He also had a turnover problem, since many people, despite his paying them good wages (above average for the type of work in order to help keep his employees), simply didn't like the idea of doing such menial work. Many felt it degrading to have to say they were janitors. I disagree with that notion because there is good money to be made in such work. My friend, for instance, was a janitor in fact, and not just in name, but in practice, and if anyone made fun of him, he could laugh about it all the way to his bank! And he did!

Still, he found that he quickly became the manager of the working staff, having to create his cleaning teams, select a leader for each, replace employees who quit, and having to assign and help deliver his workers to various sites. This isn't what my friend liked to do, but it was necessary. Yet, he no longer could just quietly work away in the night in empty buildings, listening to his music through earbuds. His sense of peace and contentment in his work had evaporated.

Peter's Principle came into full play for my friend. Although he was still competent in his new position as manager of his work teams, he did not like doing what he was doing. So beware of this problem in any idea for business, whether product or service you might develop. If you are happy doing what you are doing at the start and then your business begins to expand, you might have to make some hard choices, just as my friend did. He opted to sell the business, rather than continue doing something he no longer enjoyed. Luckily, he made another bundle doing just that.

Chapter Conclusion: Putting your idea to make money into action involves several necessary steps. You first have to really want to do what you are intending to do, find the funds and at not too high a cost to yourself or any potential business you develop, and then you must buy what you need to run the business. Once you've done that, you are ready to put your idea into action. So what comes next? Well, the next step is perseverance, as we shall see in the next chapter. However, we aren't talking about just normal perseverance here, but rather a qualified version of it.

CHAPTER THIRTEEN

Part 8— A Qualified Perseverance

When one reads self-help books, often one of the things stated in them is to have perseverance. Again, as with Napoleon Hill's Think And Grow Rich, this is so. Moreover, all these authors are right. Perseverance is key, an absolute must for many forms of self-improvement. Perseverance is also a must for making money. That much is also true.

When one comes up with an idea for making money, whether an invention, a product, a service, or whatever, usually and contrary to so many get-rich-quick stories, money doesn't instantly fall into your lap. At least, that's so in most cases. However, the premise of this book is that you can make money quickly, almost right from the start, and the prior chapters on cutting outgo, increasing income, show this well. Still, to make LOTS of money can take time. I'm not talking decades, but several years to five years or so is not uncommon.

This might seem like a long time, and to some, I suppose it is, especially those nearing retirement, or those in retirement who are just tired of "getting by," if even that. Even so, most make money using this process well before that time. As with all things, it depends on how closely you follow this advice, what idea you pick to make money, and how much of your time and effort you devote to it. The more time and effort, usually the quicker the results. For instance, very few get rich off writing just one book. Why? Well, the author is an unknown, for one. For another, his/her first work will probably be of less quality than later books. People learn as they practice, and as the old saying goes, "practice makes perfect."

There is another factor with our example of being an author. Volume. I don't mean "volume" as in the form of a book, but rather for the number of books you publish as an author. VOLUME IS THE KEY in writing. The more your write, the more books you get published, the more of a name you make for yourself, the more people who then want to read more of your books.

This means more links on the Internet, a greater amount of advertisement of all this because of those links, and so more positive results. Additionally, it means the more people who see that your books even exist. You are thus expanding your audience.

Moreover, you establish your "brand" as an author this way. If your topic is a type of nonfiction (and those types of books sell better than fiction), the more books you've written, the more you are seen as an expert on the subject, and so the more you are referred to in different places and venues, and the more books you then sell. It's an upward spiral of success.

The author who writes one book and then gives up because the sales are disappointingly low will never make money at writing. This is because he fell at the first hurdle and didn't pick his/herself up and continue to the finish line. This same idea holds true for anything you try to sell; again, this is so whether it is a product or service of any sort. So yes, perseverance is VERY important in whatever you attempt to make money at in order to increase your income.

Yet, one can go too far with this. **I AM NOT RECOMMENDING UNQUALIFIED PERSEVERANCE!** Yes, persevere, by all means. Don't let the bumps in the road to your success make you stall out on your journey to a higher income. Life may be a journey, but when it comes to success in the form of greater income, that is a destination you want to reach! Your goal might include enjoying the journey toward it, but again, your major purpose is to get there!

Therefore, if you constantly are having problems with your idea, if it just doesn't seem to be catching on, isn't making you money after you have tried every approach you can think of, then my advice is to make whatever alterations to your idea you feel you need to, or abandon the idea entirely and find a more suitable one.

This is not to say you should give up when the going gets rough! **No ride to the destination of success is an easy one.** Still, it does mean that at some point you have to decide if to continue with your idea is really going to work. You might think you've had a brilliant idea, but many people think that and wrongly. Moreover, many people will metaphorically beat themselves over the head for long periods trying to make what turns out to be an impractical idea, a success.

DON'T DO THIS! Cut your losses if you must and turn to another idea. The new idea might even be a variation of the old one, because often after we've tried the practicality of something, we see where we might have gone wrong, and so would do the job better the next time by refining that idea, making it better. Just remember, your goal is to make money, not to prove the worth of some particular idea. Keep that goal in mind at all times.

The belief that you must stick to something forever in order to make a success of it is not necessarily the way to wealth. Think of a failed idea or attempt as a learning experience and one that will help you the next time around. And there should be a next time around!

Remember, though, that you can't give up at the first hurdle that comes your way, or even the second, third, or fourth such hurdle or obstacle. Life, as in trying to increase your income, is full of such barriers. And as another old saying goes, "if you don't join the game, you can't win at it." If you just drop out of that game, you certainly won't win at it!

Therefore, you must give your idea for success your best efforts and every reasonable chance to succeed. However, it is my opinion that to continue to go on doing so, despite consistent negative results, is a waste of the most valuable commodity you possess—time! And as another famous quotation states: "Time is the stuff of life. Do not squander it."

Rather than attempt to beat the proverbial dead horse, it is my recommendation that again, you see what you've done as a lesson. Learn from your mistakes and then move on to a new idea. Of course, always give whatever you try your all. That's a necessity. To do less is self-defeating.

My point here is that you shouldn't go on giving it your all when you are banging your head against a brick wall. If you simply can't break through after seemingly endless efforts, try a different approach, a new approach, or a new product or service. Many millionaires and billionaires will tell you this. Some even go so far as to say that it was just such mistakes that guided them in the right direction to finally becoming so wealthy!

My advice is this: **FIND A WAY TO YOUR GOAL TO MAKE MORE INCOME! THIS MEANS YOU MAY HAVE TO GO OVER, UNDER, AROUND, OR EVEN THROUGH OBSTACLES.** Even as the positive thinking minister, Terry Cole-Whittaker once said, "water will always eventually find its way to the sea by doing this." So can you! Just find a way around the problems and obstacles, even if it is going for an entirely different idea!

CONCLUSION

In this book, we've covered a lot of territory and quickly. So let's reiterate what we've gone over here, and just what it takes to have the Power To Make Money! Let's begin:

First, you have to decide how badly you want money. How far are you willing to go? What are you willing to endure to get it? This holds true for not only yourself but those loved ones who will be directly affected by your actions and efforts in this regard. You and your family might have a reasonably good life now. To make a lot more money, that will probably change, because the time, effort, and costs, financially and physically will definitely be there in your climb to financial success.

So think it through very careful before you go any further! If you don't, you could end by losing everything! You should consult your spouse, children, or whomever is important in your life to see if they are willing to endure any possible hardships that making more money will entail. You don't want to end up with a divorce, for example, because your mate wasn't nearly as enthralled with the idea as you, and perhaps even resents the reduction in his/her lifestyle and relationship with you because of your need to make more money. Again, think it through!

Second, you have to ascertain where you are at the starting gate. Most of us know this pretty much already. We know if we're born with a "silver spoon in our mouths," or not. We know if we can rely on a network of wealthy relatives or not in order to get our own wealth production rolling. If you have access to people with "big bucks" to get you rolling, you can be off and running on your wealth-increasing plan almost instantly. For others of us, the vast majority, this just isn't the case.

Again, we can't help where and under what circumstances we are born. That's out of our hands. So we have to be realistic about what we can do, how we can approach something, and so go about making money. Be honest with yourself about where your position in society (class?) is, and so have a realistic idea of what it's going to take to make yourself the money you want. This is just facing reality. It doesn't mean you can't make money if you try, but it may mean you will have to try much harder than someone else. Don't let that deter you! Don't give into defeatism! Just accept your circumstances and then move on to the next step.

Third, you must take stock of your situation in realistic terms, as well. This is a direct follow through from the second step, but in this step, you focus on your assets and liabilities. If you are deep in debt, then you need to rid yourself of that burden, perhaps. Or, perhaps your plan for making money will help you to do that, so you would be sidestepping the removal of your debt burden in the interim until the money starts flowing in.

You should definitely evaluate all your assets and liabilities. These include not only monetary ones, but assets in the form of possible partners or helpers in the business, possibly valuable business contacts, or something physical you might sell in order to get the money you start your business. It might even include the idea (but be careful with this one!) of mortgaging a property you currently have paid off, or in getting a second mortgage. Again, you must carefully consider what it is you think might be an asset, and what you think might be a liability. As an example, if you have a spouse that is happy with the way things are, and is opposed to taking such risks, that's a form of liability, as well. You must take into account other people's feelings on the matter, whether they want to help, or adamantly are opposed to the whole idea.

Fourth, you must take control of your income! We went into depth on that coffee example because it is so exemplary of how you can save money without even realizing it practically, and without it adversely impacting your lifestyle to any large degree. As listed earlier, a host of things can be done to reduce your costs. **Remember, Decreasing Your Outgo Increases Your Income.** The minute you start doing that, you see your disposable income increase, not in years, but in just a matter of weeks or a month or so at the very most. The effect on your finances is almost immediate!

Fifth, if you have a debt burden that you wish to get rid of in order to have a better financial situation, or in order to go ahead with a business plan for making even more money, you should consider using one of the two methods mentioned in this book for rapidly reducing debt and so becoming debt free. These are the **Snowball Method**, and the **Avalanche Method**. Refer back to Chapter 4 for details on these approaches to reducing your debt. Remember, money freed up by removing debts is money that then can be applied to making even more money!

Sixth, think of ways of increasing your income. Whether this is as a stepping stone to get the money you need to make even more money, get out of debt, or to finance that ultimate service or product you are pinning your hopes on for making great money, or just as an end in itself, you need to increase your income.

Refer to Chapter Six to see some ideas about how to go about doing this. And remember my caveat about a second job—they have a way of becoming permanent and so perhaps adding to your problems. The burden of two jobs can have major consequences on your quality of life and family life, so be careful with that idea. Remember, you must have an end date you will stick with (and so many people end up not terminating the job at that point, so be VERY careful about that), and you must have that light at the end of the tunnel by having an end date for the second job, not only for yourself, but for your family, as well!

Seventh, you must create a business plan, come up with an idea as to how to make money to improve your lot in life permanently! Whether this is as simple as adding ever spare dollar to an ever-increasing stock portfolio that might pay dividends, supply a needed or wanted product or service, or whatever, you have to come up with an idea and plan as to how to practically go about this. You must be realistic, and consider if your idea has real value, learn how to go about doing it, and what the consequences are if you fail. You should research whatever idea it is you have as best and as thoroughly as you can!

Eighth, think about the possibility of a partnership with someone else. Again, "many hands make for light work," as "they" say. A good partner can lighten the load of the work involved in your idea and its realization, and can hurry along the process of seeing profits grow from it. Remember, one person might have to save for three years to put a deposit down on a duplex, but two people, with equal income, can probably come up with the deposit in half the time. The sooner you have that duplex (just an example), the sooner it starts earning income/profit, which can then be used for expansion and so the quicker you can buy even more properties.

However, remember my caveat about partnership, how around 80 percent of them fail, and that number could be even higher now. Friendships can be lost over such partnerships, as well. Matters can even end up in court, so consider carefully, **VERY CARE-FULLY** as to whom you pick as a partner! And remember there is more than one type of partnership. The two main ones are a **General Partnership** (where both partners might have equal say), and **Limited Partnerships**, where you might have the primary say and the other partners are just investors. My advice is to seek the advice of legal counsel if you are planning on have a partnership of any sort, and make sure such counsel draws it up as a legal document. Get it on paper and signed!

Ninth, consider the idea of maybe going it alone. You might eventually need to incorporate partners or employees as your business expands, but at the outset, at least, you don't have the worries and hassles of all that such entails. If your idea is to make money, as the woman I mentioned in Chapter 9 did by just selling bare-rooted egg trees and such on holidays, you might not need to have others involved. She did not. However, if you keep wanting your business to expand, there might come a day when you need to at least hire help, if not take on partners. Think it through.

Tenth, carefully consider your business idea to make money. Get input, from any resources available to you. Don't just say: "Hey! This is a great idea and I'm going with it!" Instead, find out what others think of your idea or plan. Talk it over. Reflect on all the factors, the pluses and minuses involved, how much work it would entail, how soon you could expect to see positive results, etc. In other words, consider carefully all aspects of your idea/plan before you proceed with it. At this point, this is your last chance to decide if you want to go ahead or consider something else, instead. It's time to "put up or shut up," as it were.

Eleventh, once you've done all this, you have reached the "doing stage." This is the biggie. After having definitely settled on your idea, you are probably going to need some money to get it going. If you don't have that money, despite trying everything earlier mentioned to increase your income and decrease your outgo, then you must seek alternative ways of finding that money. As mentioned, there are crowd sourcing websites, for example, that might work for you. A good list of them (all operable at the writing of this book) are shown in Chapter 11.

Friends and/or relatives might also be a way of finding money to start your plan in action. Perhaps you have assets you can sell to procure the startup money you need. Alternatively, you may be able to find a good loan, one with good terms and a low interest rate to get started on your plan. Personal loans, second mortgage, etc., are all possibilities. But remember the caveats! If you go this last route, you are placing yourself in debt and if your plan fails, you could be worse off than you when you started! So think through the idea of a loan from a financial institution VERY CAREFULLY! Many students have incurred large debts to pay their way through college and university. Some may have to wait decades to finish paying off the loans. Again, you don't want to end up in that type of situation, so be careful!

Twelfth, is putting your idea into actual action. You have come up with the idea. You have carefully thought it through. You have found the money by one means or another to start the business.

Now, you have to actually start doing it! This is going to take a lot of your time, talent, and effort, and it might take a while before you see results. You have to be prepared for bumps along the road. You have to consider if your family, relatives, or friends are up to the task of doing it with you.

Once started down the road to making money, you have to deal with many things. You must be prepared for this! Don't go into the idea of making money wearing rose-colored glasses. Be prepared to work long hours, and work those hours! Be prepared to deal with unexpected problems and make sure you have budgeted for them ahead of time, by having a cushion of money to get you through them. Also, remember Peter's Principle. As your enterprise grows, you will probably become more of a manager over time, an administrator, and less of a hands-on person. If this doesn't suit you, you need to find some alternative to doing these things yourself by hiring or finding someone willing to do them for you—someone you can trust!

Thirteenth, above all else, you must have a qualified perseverance. You must be willing to take the bad with the good, to persevere even when the going gets rough. However, and unlike other "rags to riches" books, I qualify that.

If you see that despite your repeated best efforts, and doing everything you can think of to do, the idea simply isn't working out, then consider letting it go. Even Elon Musk said that part of his success came directly from his failures, and that failures taught him incredibly valuable lessons. So keep that in mind, as well.

Finally, remember this last point and it is the most valuable one of all:

THE SECRET TO THE POWER TO MAKE MONEY LIES SOLELY WITHIN YOU! You are all you need to get started on the road to wealth. You, and you alone have the capability to change your circumstances, to increase your income, to expand your wealth, and to achieve your dreams! Nobody else is very likely to do this

for you. YOU MUST DO IT FOR YOURSELF AND THAT IS THE SECRET TO MAKING MONEY! So get going! Get started! And the best of luck to you in your endeavors!

END

ABOUT THE AUTHOR

Mr. McCall, like most of us, has had many ups and downs in life. He has made money, lost it, and then made it again. He has been everything from a fast-food employee, to tech writer, to real estate broker, and finally to successful writer. Along the way, he has learned what works with regard to making money and what doesn't. He often has learned this the hard way. And yes, Mr. McCall has been burdened by a heavy debt at one point in his life, so he knows what others have gone through when in deep financial straits, and are going through now. In a world torn by a Great Recession, pandemic, and Depression, the author has successfully survived financially and prospered, even when times were rough. Although, it hasn't always been easy!

By studying successful careers of others, by researching and developing the practices described in this book, the author not only found his way out of debt, but also was able to retire early and comfortably. He now owns his own home in North Carolina on two acres very close to a beautiful lake. He travels a lot, mostly to the United Kingdom where he spends up to a month at a time each year, renting a car and various cottages as he explores the beauty of the British countryside.

The author has also been to Australia, the Caribbean, Canada, Mexico, Tahiti, the Fijis, New Zealand and Europe. He makes minor trips annually, as well as always that one major, more long-term trip each year. The author has no debt to speak of, and enjoys an active lifestyle. One of his favorite things to do, though, is to sip from a glass of wine, as he watches the sun set over the rolling green hills of rural North Carolina. However, the author is planning on purchasing a second home in England, as a getaway and escape. He favors the County of Devon there, at the moment. One thing is for sure; the author is enjoying his financial freedom from debt and having a greater income. He hopes others will be able to do the same by reading this book. He also wishes to remind you that you, and you alone, have the real *Power To Make Money* for yourself! He also wishes you the best of luck in this endeavor!

PARTIAL LIST OF REFERENCES

http://www.financialsamurai.com/the-average-savings-rates-by-income-wealth-class/

https://www.freshbooks.com/blog/freelance-jobs/

https://www.delawareinc.com/blog/general-partnership-vs-limited-partnership/

https://www.google.com/search?client=firefox-b-1-d&q=what+is+the+avalanche+method+of+debt+reduction%3F

https://www.daveramsey.com/blog/how-to-pay-off-debt?utm_source=google&utm_id=go_cmp-959054304_adg-80309682441_ad-374157147305_kwd-19729566209_dev-c_ext-_prd-&gclid=CjwKCAjw97P5BRBQEiwAGflV6UJIAvM0GeyUP38bKxhBWZ5oen0GFuf4M-7bIG-T2BJ3Jn1i8XMGYBoCJrIQAvD_BwE

https://www.entrepreneur.com/article/298348

https://www.thesimpledollar.com/make-money/how-to-make-money/

https://www.google.com/search?client=firefox-b-1-d&sxsrf=ALeKk03tVb0t6J5I7RnSmrlPgZJU2DEKWg%3A1596894821176&lei=Za4uX9WsCuzAytMP4YWdgAE&q=get%20paid%20to%20search%20the%20web&ved=2ahUKEwiV87zk4IvrAhVsoHIEHeFCBxAQsKwBKAB6BAgdEAE&biw=1366&bih=626

https://www.forbes.com/sites/jrose/2018/04/24/make-money-online/#87b674449541

https://thecollegeinvestor.com/22720/make-money-from-home/

https://www.businessnewsdaily.com/4686-how-to-start-a-business.html

https://www.nerdwallet.com/blog/small-business/

https://www.entrepreneur.com/article/201588

https://www.lifehack.org/818977/how-to-start-a-company

https://medium.com/thrive-global/7-powerful-habits-of-self-made-billionaires-that-will-immediately-improve-your-life-dd37215706ee

https://www.businessinsider.com/billionaire-study-six-habits-success-building-wealth-2019-6

http://financialchase.com/10-billionaire-habits-you-can-start-today/

https://www.entrepreneur.com/article/307250

https://www.shopify.com/blog/crowdfunding

https://review.chicagobooth.edu/economics/2017/article/never-mind-1-percent-lets-talk-about-001-percent

https://www.brookings.edu/blog/up-front/2019/06/25/six-facts-about-wealth-in-the-united-states/

https://whorulesamerica.ucsc.edu/power/wealth.html

https://www.earlytorise.com/how-to-play-and-win-the-game-of-making-money/

https://www.scottyoung.com/blog/2008/06/03/why-making-money-is-more-fun-than-having-it/

https://www.huffpost.com/entry/what-you-need-to-know-abo_32_b_8884646

https://projectlifemastery.com/game-of-money/